WRITING
SKILLS
HANDBOOK

WRITING SKILLS HANDBOOK

Fourth Edition

Charles Bazerman
University of California, Santa Barbara

Harvey S. Wiener
Adelphi University

Houghton Mifflin Company   Boston   New York

Senior Sponsoring Editor: Dean Johnson
Development Editor: Mary Furlong Healey
Project Editor: Elena Di Cesare
Editorial Assistant: Angela Schoenherr
Senior Production/Design Coordinator: Jennifer Waddell
Senior Manufacturing Coordinator: Marie Barnes
Senior Marketing Manager: Nancy Lyman

Printed in the U.S.A.

Library of Congress Catalog Card Number: 97-72440

ISBN: 0-395-86811-4

123456789-QF-01 00 99 98 97

Contents

To the Instructor

To write with confidence, a student needs to know the rules of grammar and usage. In *Writing Skills Handbook,* Fourth Edition, we present rules and advice about the matters of grammar and usage students most frequently need help with. The first half of the text offers advice on the processes, purposes, style, and organization of writing; the second half presents rules of sentence form, grammar, punctuation, spelling, and other mechanics. The advice and rules are presented concisely, avoiding grammatical terms and rhetorical theory wherever possible. The text is organized clearly: charts and checklists and the system of reference numbers make the book easy to use. Overall, the presentation allows the student to use the book independently, leaving the instructor free to explore more advanced writing issues with the class.

The Fourth Edition includes a separate chapter on writing from sources; additional material on sentence style, relative pronouns, and homonyms; and expanded coverage of adjectives and prepositions.

A supplementary package, available upon adoption, consists of exercise material offering practice of skills. The package includes three forms of diagnostic tests on duplicating masters. These tests are also available on computer disks.

C.B
H.S.W.

To the Student

This handbook is designed to be useful to you. Think of it not as a set of rules to memorize but as a reference that will help guide you through the writing process. Use it when you feel you need help planning your writing, for example, or deciding how to phrase a passage, how to select the right form of a word, or how to punctuate a complicated sentence. It can also help you understand the corrections your teacher may ask you to make. Look up information only as you need it to improve your skills.

The handbook offers several ways of easily finding the information you need as you write, revise, or edit your papers, and as you review your teacher's comments and suggestions. The detailed table of contents identifies each topic covered, and a summary of the contents is provided on the inside back cover. The topics are numbered so you can locate them quickly on the page; the heads running along the top of each page also guide you to the material you seek. Use the correction chart on the inside front cover to turn directly to appropriate numbered sections. The detailed index will also help you find the precise page location of specific items. Over thirty lists and charts present information quickly and clearly.

The explanations in this book are straightforward and nontechnical and are accompanied by pertinent examples. They should enable you to understand all the rules of grammar and usage on your own without a teacher's help.

C.B.
H.S.W.

Acknowledgments

We are grateful to the following reviewers, who made many helpful suggestions: John Bell, York University, Ontario, Canada; Carol Gregory, Wilberforce University, OH; Conne Hollander, Oakland Community College—Highland Lakes Campus, MI; Roger Pearson, Providence College, RI; Dean Rehberger, Michigan State University; Deborah Vanderbilt, St. John Fisher College, NY.

UNIT ONE

Composition

1

The Writing Process

When you talk, you say your words and sentences once, and that's it—you can't go back and change what your listener has already heard. But when you write, you have plenty of time and plenty of chances to work on your words before your reader sees them. In your rough drafts (a **draft** is an early working copy of writing) you can change your mind: you can put in things you left out the first time, you can try to make your message clearer, and you can even stop for a while to collect your thoughts. The reader of your final copy sees only the neat results—not the messy work that went into making them.

Good writing takes time—time for thinking, time for making changes, time for polishing details. To be as good as it can be, a piece of writing should go through a number of stages before it is finished. The stages vary for different types of papers and for different people, of course, because everybody has his or her own way of working. And all writers find at times that they jump back and forth from earlier to later stages in a particular piece of writing. In other words, you should not feel locked in to a fixed way of working. Nonetheless, moving through the following stages will help you improve your writing process.

1a   GATHERING IDEAS

1a(1)   Getting the First Idea

Getting the first idea takes time and patience. Never start writing until you have thought about your topic for a while. If you don't get any good ideas right away, relax: maybe an idea will come to you later when you are walking home or eating dinner. Even if you have only an hour for an in-class assignment, think about your topic for a few minutes before you begin to write.

3

Usually, an instructor assigns a general topic for the paper, and you have to find a specific part of the topic to write on. At times, though, you will be asked to find a topic by yourself. Then you will be both lucky and unlucky—lucky because you can write on anything that interests you, and unlucky because making all the decisions is hard work. If the choice is yours, use it; pick a topic you will really enjoy.

When the instructor assigns a topic, your challenge is to find things you know about and are interested in that relate to the topic. You have to question yourself to find out what you have to say on the matter. The following questions will help you find ideas to write about, based on what you already know and think.

Questions for Finding Ideas

▶ *How many different subjects are included under the general topic?* "Sports" includes baseball, football, tennis, Ping-Pong, hockey, and many other games.

▶ *Do you have any personal knowledge about any part of the topic? Can you tell a true story that relates to the assignment?* If you ever worked for a corporation, you probably know many things that will help you with the topic "How Companies Are Organized." How many bosses did you have? Who was responsible to whom? How much did rank count and how did you gain rank? What tasks did each department perform?

▶ *Do you have an opinion or feeling about any part of the topic? Can you back up that opinion or feeling?* You may have no interest in and no knowledge of the topic "The Future of the Internet" except for your exasperation at all the claims that the Internet is the most revolutionary technology since the wheel. Personally, you find it no more exciting than the marketing of a new color of fingernail polish. You can use your memory of all the exaggerated and exasperating commentaries about the Internet to write that the only sure thing about its future is that there will continue to be overblown accounts and overinflated claims.

▶ *Do you know of a book, newspaper or magazine article, movie, or TV show that relates to any part of the topic? Does it give you any ideas?* Perhaps your local newspaper has been publishing stories about difficulties faced by immigrant families in your community or about local factories that have been relying on immigrant labor—stories that will give you some help in developing your own ideas on "Immigration and the American Economy."

There are other methods that will help you explore your thoughts and feelings in order to develop ideas for writing. These methods, described below, can be used for specific topics or more open-ended assignments.

Freewriting is exactly what it sounds like. You take a blank piece of paper and just begin writing freely, without worrying where your writing is going or how it will look. You don't have to worry about how other people will judge your freewriting, because no one but you will ever have to see it. The freewriting is not your final essay, but only a way of talking to yourself on paper.

As you talk to yourself on paper, you will start to remember things, identify feelings, and develop ideas that you will be able to use in your essay. After you finish freewriting, you can then read over what you have written to pick out those parts that may be helpful for your formal assignment.

Here, for example, is how one student began freewriting after the teacher had asked the students to describe a time when they were treated unfairly.

> It's so hot today. Why is he making us write when it's so hot? What does he want us to write about, anyway? Being unfair. It's all unfair. Life's unfair. School's unfair. You know what's really unfair? The way they make you register. Can't get the courses you want. Can't get times you can live with. It's such chaos. You don't even know what's going on, and you just get stuck with a program. That's it. Registration. What's unfair about it.

The student now has an idea for the paper. The idea is still very rough, and details have to be developed. But the student has found something about which she has a lot of information and strong feelings to draw on.

A **writing journal** is a notebook in which you can freewrite every day. By writing down things you see, experience, or think about, you can build up many ideas for writing. When the instructor makes an assignment, you will already have a record of many ideas that interest you. Even more important, through your daily practice in the journal, your ideas for writing will have grown deeper and richer. Many professional writers keep journals to develop their ideas for writing.

Brainstorming is a kind of group freewriting out loud. A small group of people throw out ideas rapidly to one another, without worrying about how good the ideas are. Once people's imaginations get warmed up, the ideas are likely to become better and better. One person's ideas may trigger another person's thinking, and pretty soon ideas are flying back and forth.

One good way to get a brainstorming session going is to ask the group to describe the problem they need to solve. As people start talking about the problem, they develop a better picture of exactly what they need to do to solve it. By defining the problem, they are also starting to define a solution. For example, a group of students who use brainstorming on the assignment about unfairness might have the following conversation.

> —Unfairness . . . unfairness.
> —What's unfairness?
> —You know, that's when someone does something to you that you don't like.
> —No, some things you don't like are still fair. Does a criminal like going to jail? But that's fair.
> —It's more like someone does something that doesn't take your rights or feelings or needs into account.
> —I don't know, maybe. But why does the teacher want us to write this? What's the problem he wants us to solve?
> —Well, we've been describing things. Maybe he just wants us to have practice describing things?
> —OK, we have to find something good to describe . . . like with a lot of details, and sort of dramatic. But then why didn't he just tell us to describe any incident?
> —Yeah. Maybe he wanted us to think about ideas like unfairness.
> —Right. So then the event should really show something about what unfairness is.
> —Just complaining, like about registration, won't be good enough. We'll have to show why it's unfair, or what it tells about unfairness, or how it fits with some idea about unfairness.
> —You mean, like when my brother got to go to Chicago and I had to stay back. I mean it really wasn't unfair, because I had to keep up with gymnastics training, but I felt it was unfair, and those feelings of unfairness made me angry and I tried to get him in trouble so he couldn't go. I guess I was being unfair. So I could write about what happens with the feelings of unfairness—how maybe they create more unfairness.

Talking over the problem of the paper gave the students a much better idea about what they had to do. With a better definition of the problem, they started to find more interesting ideas to write about.

1a(2)   Limiting the Idea and Making It Precise

Even though it may be interesting, your first idea is likely to be vague. The idea may also be too big for the length of the paper you are writing. You have to decide exactly what you are going to write about your subject and how you are going to limit it. If, for example, your first idea is to write about a car accident you were in, you may want to focus on the terrible attitude of the driver of the other car because that is the most interesting, most focused part of the story.

The following questions will help you limit your final topic and make it more precise.

Questions for Limiting a Topic

▶ *Who will read this paper?* You would write different things for your teacher, your classmates, your parents, or the readers of your college newspaper. You would have to explain to your little sister many things that your friends would already understand. Your music teacher and your history teacher are looking for different kinds of information.

▶ *What is the purpose of the paper?* Are you giving a recipe for beef stew or are you giving directions for putting together a table? Are you persuading the reader to vote for you? Are you showing your teacher that you know what a corporation is? Are you telling a funny story?

▶ *Do you know enough about the topic to write about it? If not, can you find out enough before the assignment is due?* You can always write better if you know a lot about your subject. You will have more things to say because you will know what is important. You will know what should be left out, and you will know the words, phrases, and organization to use. Even when assigned a topic you think you know nothing in particular about (like "Problems in America"), you can usually bend the topic to something you know. For example, if your little brother goes to kindergarten, you could change the topic to "Problems in Early Childhood Education." If many people you know have lost their jobs, you could write on "What Unemployment Is Doing to My Neighborhood." If you fish for a hobby, you can write on "Sports Fishing and Protecting the Environment."

▶ *Are you interested in the topic?* The more interest you have, the more effort you will put into finding good ways to explain your subject. But don't use lack of interest as an excuse for not writing. You can almost always hit on something of interest that fits the general topic. The assignment "Describe an object" might leave you cold, but you can still choose the object to write about—that flashy pair of new shoes you have been thinking of buying or that fuel pump you just fixed. Remember also that some subjects that look dull grow more interesting as you work on them.

▶ *Is your subject too big or too little for the length of the paper?* Don't try to tell the story of your life in one paragraph or what you had for breakfast in ten pages. Generally, a paragraph can hold only one fairly simple and specific idea—a description of one event, one person, or one object, an explanation of one point, or proof of one opinion. A longer essay requires a subject with several parts or ideas that fit together to make a single overall point.

In one paragraph on "My Part-Time Job," you could write only a short description of the place of work, the duties, the pay, and the hours. In an essay of four or five paragraphs, you might write in detail about the skills you needed and have learned, the friends and enemies you have made, the ways the job affects your school life, the strange things that happen on the job, and the chance for promotion once you get your degree.

A good topic is important, but don't waste too much time trying to find one. The choice of a topic is just the first of many choices you will have to make—about main points, about details, about organization, about language. If you take too much time finding the topic, you won't have enough time to do everything else properly. Remember, a reasonable topic, even if it isn't the greatest, is better than no topic.

1a(3) Building on the First Idea

Depending on the type of writing, the time it takes to build up ideas can be ten minutes or a month. If you are writing a short, in-class paragraph, all you need to do is jot down on a piece of scrap paper the details that support your topic sentence (see **2b**). If you are writing a full-length research paper, you will need several weeks to take careful notes from a number of books and articles.

Talking with a friend, classmate, or relative about your topic is very useful. Other people can help you anticipate the kinds of questions readers may have about your topic. They can also help you judge whether your ideas for the piece of writing will make sense to a reader. Simply putting your ideas together verbally to explain them to someone else will help you clarify your thoughts, even if the other person does not say anything in response.

1b PLANNING

Once you have the topic, ideas, and details in mind and in your notes, you must then decide how you are going to pull all this material together. You must face questions like:

▶ How many paragraphs do I need?
▶ In what order shall I put the ideas?
▶ What is the best type of paragraph for the purpose I have in mind? (See **2c** and **2d**.)
▶ What details go with what main points?

You also might want to make an outline (see **3c**) to help yourself plan.

1c WRITING AND REWRITING

1c(1) The First Draft

Only now, after all the work of gathering ideas and planning, do you begin to write. The main point of a first draft is to get your ideas down in words, sentences, and paragraphs without worrying too much about them. Try to write the first draft straight through. Finish it. Don't get stuck on a difficult phrase or a complex idea. Don't worry about spelling or other problems you may have. You can always go back and change things later. You will feel much better once the first draft is finished. You will know that you have something—something that will need more work, some changes, some smoothing out—but nonetheless *something* on paper.

Now, if you have time, put aside the first draft for a while. You will find when you return to it that your mind is fresher and that you will have a better view of the whole paper. Also, try to get someone else to read your draft. A reader can help you see the strengths and weaknesses in your paper.

You'll want to think about how to develop ideas, details, logic, and organization when you reread your first draft. You should ask yourself the following questions.

First Draft Revision Questions

▶ Does the writing as a whole make sense?
▶ Did I leave anything out?
▶ Should things be in a different order?
▶ Should I build up or explain anything more?
▶ Should I give more or better details and examples?
▶ Should I leave out any part?
▶ Can I write a stronger beginning or ending?

Mark up your first draft with the necessary changes. Cross out whole paragraphs; put arrows to show where you are moving sentences; write new sentences in the margins and on extra pages. Write notes to yourself. To a stranger, the corrected first draft may look like a mess! To you, of course, it should make sense.

1c(2)   The Second Draft

Make a fresh copy of your first draft so that you can easily read the revised version. In the process, you may find further corrections you wish to make. Reread this second draft. Ask yourself the following questions.

Second Draft Revision Questions

▶   Can I rewrite any sentences to make them clearer?

▶   Are my most important phrases and statements in the most important places in sentences and paragraphs?

▶   Can I put less important statements in less important places?

▶   Are there any mistakes in grammar, sentence structure, punctuation, or spelling?

In examining your sentences to improve them, you may want to consider the following principles of sentence style.

Sentence Revision Questions

▶   Do the main subject and verb of each sentence convey the most important information?

▶   Do the sentences express the ideas as concisely as possible? Do they contain any unnecessary words?

▶   Have I used *there is* or *there are* in too many of my sentences? Are there other empty phrases I can eliminate?

▶   Do any of my sentences have passive verbs? Would those sentences be more effective with active verbs? (See pages 83–84.)

▶   Do my sentences contain any unnecessary slang, jargon, or unusually lengthy words? Would more familiar words serve as well or better?

▶   Can my word choices be more precise or lively?

▶   Are the sentences all of the same length or pattern? Can I vary the sentence length and style? Can I combine sentences to improve the effect? (See pages 64–68.)

▶   Are parallel ideas expressed in parallel grammatical forms? (See pages 72–73.)

Again, after you make all your corrections, the second draft will look like a mess. If you've been keeping a record of your usual mistakes, now is the time to examine it. If you know what your errors usually are, you can more easily avoid them.

1c(3) Writing with Word Processors

Word processing makes revision much simpler, as you can quickly see the effects of the changes you make and you need not retype an entire essay every time you wish to alter a part of it. You can incorporate notes and phrases from your early idea sketches into later drafts. You can rewrite your outline, filling in sections as you go. You can experiment with rearranging parts and print out a clean-looking copy at each stage. No matter how many changes you make, you always have a readable version in front of you.

However, the ease with which you can transfer phrases, change paragraphs around, and print out clean copy whenever you wish also has dangers. Because you do not rewrite the whole essay at each stage, you never have to read through every word carefully in order. This means you could easily neglect to work through all the parts equally. By focusing too closely on one section, you may miss poorly written sentences on another page. You may change one part without thinking about other parts that might have to be changed to fit. You might build up one section in the middle so much that it overpowers the rest of the essay.

When you write with a word processor, you should do the following things.

▶ Go over your drafts carefully, thinking about each word and how it relates to the whole essay.
▶ Print out the draft several times during the writing process, so you can get a sense of how the essay looks as a whole.
▶ Mark corrections on the hard copy before going back to make final revisions onscreen.
▶ Use programs that check your spelling and grammar. Do not rely totally on them, however. They do not find all errors.
▶ Proofread carefully, using hard copy.

1d PREPARING THE FINAL COPY

1d(1) Typing or Writing for Legibility

Make your final copy neat and easy to read. This is likely to be the only copy your teacher and other readers will ever see. This copy is what you submit, what someone will judge you on. People are much more willing to read your words if they do not have to struggle through a sea of smudges and a jungle of cross-outs. Whether or not you think it's fair, the good appearance of a paper may make a difference in your grade. On your rough draft make whatever mess you want; on the final copy make your best impression. Of course, if you have been revising your drafts on a word processor, it will be easy for you to produce a neat final version.

Most writers prepare their final copy following the suggestions in the chart on page 13. (Your teacher may have more specific directions.)

1d(2) Proofreading for Mistakes

If you have worked carefully through the previous steps, the final copy should have relatively few mistakes; however, you should read through it with care to make sure you didn't miss anything or make corrections inaccurately. If you need to correct only a few small things, correct them neatly by drawing a single ink line through words that are to be left out or by using a good ink or typewriter eraser and erasing neatly. You can use a small caret ∧ if you have to add words. A single slanted line / separates words that should have space between them. If many errors need correction, recopy the paper—even though you don't want to! If you use a word processor, print out a corrected, clean copy.

1d(3) Learning from Comments

A teacher reads your paper and makes comments so that you can improve your writing. He or she shows you where you went wrong, where you could better develop your points, where your paper really succeeds. If you take the comments seriously, your writing will improve. Many teachers will allow you to rewrite your papers to raise your grades. Some demand a rewrite as an assignment. In some schools, writing teachers hold conferences with their students to go over the corrections and to discuss ways to improve the papers.

In any case, you will learn more if you read and understand each correction and rewrite the corrected passages, making the suggested improvements. If you don't understand the teacher's comment—what it means, what you did wrong, what you should be doing—*ask* your teacher. Unless you know how to correct your errors, you will probably make them again on your next paper.

WHAT YOUR FINAL COPY SHOULD LOOK LIKE

	If It Is Typed or Word Processed	*If It Is Handwritten*
Paper	8½ × 11 inches, white, unlined, sturdy; separated sheets of continuous computer paper	8½ × 11 inches, white, wide lines
Ink	Use black ink.	Use black or blue-black ink.
Spacing	Double-space.	Use ruled lines.
Margins	Leave at least 1 inch at top, bottom, and on each side. Remove paper strips from edges of computer paper.	Use ruled margins at top and left. Leave 1 inch on right. Skip two or three lines at the bottom.
Name and Date	Place at top of page 1 or on a title page.	
Title	Center at top of page 1 or on a title page. Do not use quotation marks. Do not underline. Skip line after the title.	
Paragraphs	Indent five spaces.	Indent 1 inch.
Page Numbers	Use Arabic numerals (2, 3, 4, . . .). Start numbering on page 2, placing the number at the top center or top right-hand corner.	
Neatness	Avoid strike-outs, cross-outs, ink smudges, and erasure tears. Separate computer paper evenly and without tearing.	Use a plain, readable handwriting. Avoid cross-outs, ink blots, and erasure tears.

You'll also want to keep a record of your errors somewhere in your notebook, especially in regard to your spelling mistakes.

Your teacher will surely explain how his or her marking system works, but most teachers' comments are of two types: overall comments written at the end of the paper and specific suggestions made in the margins next to your sentences. Overall comments might be about style, organization, or some smaller error that you keep repeating. The overall comments might discuss some point you make, or they may suggest an idea for further thought or more reading on the subject. Your instructor's marginal comments usually deal with things such as sentence mistakes, unclear meanings, word choice, spelling, and punctuation. On the inside front cover of this book is a list of symbols that many teachers use to make specific corrections in the margins of students' papers. Your instructor may add his or her own particular marks to these.

STEPS IN A WRITTEN ASSIGNMENT: A REVIEW

▶ Getting the first idea
▶ Building up ideas by thinking, gathering notes, and talking to people
▶ Planning
▶ Writing the first draft and asking someone to read and comment on it
▶ Changing the first draft to develop ideas, details, logic, and organization
▶ Writing the second draft
▶ Fixing the second draft to improve the language
▶ Writing the final, clean copy
▶ Proofreading
▶ Learning from an instructor's comments

2

The Paragraph

A **paragraph** is a group of sentences (usually three to fifteen) about the same topic. A paragraph can be a separate piece of writing in itself or it can be part of a longer piece such as an essay or a chapter of a book.

To start a paragraph, begin on a fresh line and indent the first line of the paragraph one inch (or five typed spaces) from the left margin. All the other lines in the paragraph should start at the left margin. After the end of the last sentence of the paragraph, leave the rest of the line blank.

To write clear, well-developed, well-organized paragraphs:

▶ Have something to say.
▶ Write about one thing and tell the reader what that is.
▶ Explain and support your statements with specific details.
▶ Put the sentences in a logical order.
▶ Connect your ideas clearly.
▶ Don't cut your paragraph too short and don't let it drag on too long.

How long should a paragraph be? Long enough to develop the topic fully, but not so long that it repeats itself or starts a new topic. The following questions should help you decide if your paragraph is the right length.

Determining Paragraph Length

Unless you can answer yes to the following questions, your paragraph is too short.

▶ Have I explained my topic sentence completely?
▶ Have I given enough examples or supporting details?
▶ Have I been specific enough?

▶ Have I done everything I promised in my topic sentence?
▶ Have I completed everything I started?

If you answer yes to the next questions, your paragraph may be too long.

▶ Have I started on a new topic by mistake?
▶ Have I said everything completely, and am I just repeating myself using different words?
▶ Do the extra examples add something new, or are they just showing the same thing I said before?
▶ Is there so much in the paragraph that the reader will get confused?

2a   WRITING THE TOPIC SENTENCE

The **topic sentence** tells the main idea of the paragraph. All the sentences of a paragraph should offer information about that main idea. The topic sentence should be very clear, to the point, and easy to find, because you don't want to hide your main idea from the reader. For this reason, the topic sentence should usually be the first sentence of the completed paragraph.

In the topic sentence you should state the topic and your focus or point of view. In addition to stating the topic, you must make clear why you are talking about the topic, what your attitude is, and what you are trying to illustrate.

The topic sentence is a kind of promise. If you say, "There are three good ways to get a date" in your topic sentence, but you don't describe these three ways, the reader will be disappointed.

Sometimes, of course, you do change the topic of a paragraph as you write it. Halfway through the paragraph on dating, you may realize that there are four ways or that there is no good way. Then you must go back and rewrite the topic sentence so that it correctly tells the reader what to find in the paragraph.

To write good topic sentences:

▶ State the topic clearly—so both you and the reader will know what you're talking about.
▶ Limit the topic—so that you will not have too much to talk about.

▶ Give the topic a focus or point of view—so the reader will know why you are writing about the topic.

▶ Make sure you have a complete, correct sentence—so that you can use it as the first sentence of the finished paragraph.

The kind of topic sentence you write also depends on the kind of paragraph you want to write. (In **2c** and **2d** you will learn about different ways to develop ideas in a paragraph.) If, for example, you wanted to write about dating by describing a date you'd had, you would want one kind of topic sentence. If, however, you preferred to give directions on how to get a date, you'd need a different topic sentence.

The table on pages 20–21 will help you see how different kinds of topic sentences suit the special demands of paragraph patterns.

2b   ADDING SUPPORTING DETAILS

A topic sentence alone does not make up a whole paragraph. You need specific details to explain, support, and develop your first sentence.

The following two examples, written by two different students about the same experience, make the importance of well-chosen, specific details very clear. The first student, Wilma, writes in general terms; the few details she uses do not seem important. It is not easy to see exactly what the point of her story is.

Lunch

Glenda and I went to lunch at the coffee shop. We had a very nasty waiter. He was so slow. He finally took our order. I had a hamburger, French fries, and a milk shake. Glenda had a tuna fish sandwich, coffee, and a piece of pie.

Glenda, on the other hand, brings out the point of the story with specific details. She lets you know what she and her friend felt, what they saw, what they did, and what they said. You can really picture what happened. Even the details of what they ate take on a special meaning.

Lunch at Jerry's

When Wilma and I lunched at Jerry's Coffee Shop during last week's snowstorm, the waiter treated us as if we were worse than nothing, but we showed him! We shoved our way into the crowded shop just after noon: men and women in wet coats filled the tables and more stood waiting. Finally a fat lady with a giant red hat and her noisy daughter left and the two of us jumped into their seats, which were still warm. Their dirty plates, crumpled napkins, and half-eaten pickles covered the table. Fifteen minutes later, when the waiter still hadn't come to clear up and take our orders, Wilma yelled out to him, as he was serving the people next to us, "How about cleaning this up?" The waiter mumbled a promise to return, but he vanished into the kitchen. Fifteen minutes later he returned, took away the garbage, gave the wooden tabletop two wipes, and threw two menus onto the wet table. And then he had the nerve to say we had to show him our money before we ordered! Wilma put on a big phony smile and said, "What's the matter, honey? Ain't you never seen a black girl's money before?" We took out our purses bulging with those extra dollars we brought to buy our textbooks. Wilma did the ordering then. I just snickered while she said in her most sugar-sweet voice. "Well, I'll just have a little hamburger, some French fries, and a triple-thick chocolate milk shake. My friend here will have a tuna fish sandwich, coffee, and a piece of apple pie . . . maybe put some ice cream on that pie . . . and some whipped cream . . . maybe a cherry on top." We laughed at the miserable waiter through the whole meal.

2b(1)   Finding Details

There are many different kinds of details you can use. The table on page 22 may give you some ideas. Which kind you use depends on the kind of story you are trying to tell or the kind of point you are trying to make. In the example above, details of sight and sound bring out the miserable atmosphere in Jerry's Coffee Shop, while details of the food ordered bring out the students' feelings of pride. Statistics about lunch-counter sales, although detailed, would not particularly help the point of that story.

2b(2)   Selecting Details

Just having details, of course, isn't enough; you must have the right details and in the right amount. The details must show what you want to show, make clear what you want to make clear. If the details have little to do with your point, you waste time and paper. Even if all the details fit, you can still lose the reader by using too many. One exactly right detail is better than a boring list.

Therefore, after you think of many possible details to support your topic sentence, you must choose the most useful and throw away the rest. In looking over the details, you may even find one that supports your point so well that you don't need any others. For instance, in listing all the times your father was kind, you may remember the one Christmas when your family was out of money and he took on an extra job just to get gifts for the family. Don't feel bad if you don't use all the details you struggled to find; if you hadn't gone through them all, you would never have found the one you wanted.

Questions for Choosing Details
► Does the detail support the topic sentence?
► Is the detail the clearest example of what you want to show?
► Is the detail specific enough?
► Is the detail lively and interesting? Could you find another that shows the same thing but is more interesting?
► Does the detail tie together several things you want to say?

To develop telling details, follow these suggestions:

► Read your topic sentence.
► List all the details you can think of that support the topic sentence. Try to be as specific as possible. Don't worry that you will have too many details. You won't use them all.
► Choose the details that support your point best.
► Look at how all the details you pick fit together. Ask yourself whether the details you pick repeat the same idea without adding anything new to the overall impression. Can you cut down on the number of details and still have the same effect?
► Reread the topic sentence. Can you make it sharper as a result of the details you have developed?
► See whether the details and the sharper topic sentence give you ideas for even better details.

2c   ARRANGING THE SUPPORTING DETAILS

You cannot throw the topic sentence and supporting details together in just any order. The reader will not be able to tell what your point is or how the details relate to the topic sentence. Therefore, you must put your material together in an order that is easy to follow and that fits the point you are trying to make.

SOME TYPES OF TOPIC SENTENCES

Purpose of the Paragraph	*Things to Include in the Topic Sentence*	
	Subject	*Focus*
To tell a story	What happened	Basic facts—who, where, when, how
To tell a personal experience	What happened; time; place	The importance of the experience; how you felt
To describe	The time or person; time, place	The main overall impression
To give directions	The task you will explain	The most important thing you must do
To argue or persuade	A person, place, or thing	Your opinion about that thing (use words like *should, ought, good, bad, better, worse*)
To offer a solution	The problem	The solution
To define a word or term	The word or term to be defined	The general category it belongs to and what makes it different from the rest of the category
To analyze or classify	The thing being classified or analyzed	The groups or parts that make it up
To compare or contrast	The two items to be compared	The main thing learned by the comparison
To explain a cause and effect	What happened	A suggestion that you will explain *why*
To explain a process	The process to be explained	An overview of the steps in the process

Example

One Thursday last month in the college cafeteria, seven young men planned a prank that turned the entire college upside down.

Four years ago, in November, when my parents sent me an airline ticket from Belize to New York City so that I could join them, I was scared and unsure of my future.

My block, at Avenue M and East 19th Street, is an exciting place to live.

To make a good Italian spaghetti sauce, a beginning cook must have patience.

Teenagers should be more outspoken about protecting their rights.

In order to decrease crime in our apartment building, we must set up a tenant patrol.

"Getting over" is the practical skill of succeeding in difficult situations.

In any type of gambling there are three important factors: the original money paid (or the "bet"), the chance involved, and the "payoff."

When I compare my elementary school today with what it was like when I went there ten years ago, I see that there is much more learning going on now.

Many small businesses have had to shut down this winter for a number of reasons.

Producing a book requires the cooperation of author, editor, designer, printer, and distributor.

SOME TYPES OF DETAIL

	Examples
Sensory	
sight	*gray, rectangular, massive, grimy*
smell	*foul-smelling, scent of day-old cabbage*
taste	*the slightly acid taste of polluted air*
touch	*rough and irregular abrasiveness of concrete blocks*
hearing	*the constant drone of machinery*
Emotional impact	*depressing, nerve-shattering*
Statistics	*an unemployment rate of 17.3 percent*
Facts	*Jim had not seen his father for twelve years.*
Incidents	*Jim's anger boiled over the day that . . .*
Quotations	*"Hate oppression, but fear the oppressed."—V. S. Naipaul*

There are several ways to arrange information in a paragraph. Your topic sentence will often make very clear what kind of organization to use. For example, if your topic sentence is "The day I broke my leg skiing was awful from the moment I woke up," you will probably begin at the beginning of the event and describe each thing in the order in which it happened (time order).

Sometimes a paragraph can be arranged in different ways. You have to decide which seems to be clearest and most to the point. For example, you could describe how gorgeous your new motorcycle is by

▶ starting at the front wheel and working back (space order).
▶ starting with the parts that are nice and working up to the really beautiful stuff, leaving the best for last (order of importance).

2c(1) Time Order

Uses: to tell stories and incidents, to give a history or series of events, to give step-by-step directions.

How to use it: start at the beginning and tell the events in the order in which they happened.

> In the 1940's, civil rights leaders began a struggle against discrimination and segregation. Leaders of the movement turned to the federal courts, and, in a series of cases beginning in 1941, the Supreme Court ruled against various forms of segregation. A Supreme Court decision in 1954—*Brown v. Board of Education of Topeka*—overturned an 1896 Court decision that allowed "separate but equal" schools for black students. The court ordered schools to end segregation with "all deliberate speed." Resistance to this decision forced President Eisenhower to send federal troops to Arkansas in 1957 to protect black students. In the early 1960's, President Kennedy used federal marshals in Mississippi and National Guard units in Alabama to ensure that black students were allowed to enter state universities.
>
> —Marvin Perry

2c(2)   Space Order

Uses: to describe people, places, and things.

How to use it: decide on the best space order for the subject (top to bottom, front to back, clockwise, or other). Once you start a pattern, use it for all the objects in the space. Do not break off in the middle.

> In a little while we had come to the top of the ridge where, looking to the east, you can see for the first time the monument and the burying ground on the little hill where the church is. That is where the terrible thing started. Just south of the burying ground on the little hill a deep dry gulch runs about east and west, very crooked, and it rises westward to nearly the top of the ridge where we were. It had no name, but the Wasichus sometimes call it Battle Creek now. We stopped on the ridge not far from the head of the dry gulch. Wagon-guns were still going off over there on the little hill, and they were going off again where they hit along the gulch. There was much shooting down yonder, and there were many cries, and we could see cavalrymen scattered over the hills ahead of us. Cavalrymen were riding along the gulch and shooting into it, where the women and children were running away and trying to hide in the gullies and the stunted pines.
>
> —Black Elk

2c(3)   Order of Importance

Uses: to describe, to impress, to persuade.

How to use it: start with the least important details and lead up to the most important and impressive ones.

> After 20 years of sorting through garbage cans and landfills, the archaeologist William L. Rathje has accumulated precious memories. There are the 40-year-old hot dogs, perfectly preserved beneath dozens of strata of waste, and the head of lettuce still in pristine condition after 25 years. But the hands-down winner, the one that still makes him shake his head in disbelief, is an order of guacamole he recently unearthed. Looking like it had just been mixed, it sat next to a newspaper apparently thrown out the same day. The date was 1967.
> —William Grimes

2d   OTHER PARAGRAPH PATTERNS

Ideas and information can be organized in many ways. The following paragraph patterns are frequently used.

2d(1)   Definition

Uses: to make clear the meaning of a word, to explore exactly what a thing is, or to give a new, original meaning of a word.

How to use it: the topic sentence should be a basic definition. The following sentences should explain difficult parts of the definition; give examples; contrast the thing being defined with other things of its general type; and describe the thing more exactly.

> Sickle cell anemia is an inherited disease that occurs when the hemoglobin in red blood cells changes its structure. Hemoglobin is the substance in red blood cells that carries oxygen throughout the body. When the hemoglobin changes its structure, the red blood cells take on a sickle-shaped form, giving the disease its name. The changes in the red blood cells lead to a variety of symptoms: attacks of pain (called sickle cell crises), weakness, jaundice, and leg ulcers. The disease also often lowers resistance to other diseases. Some people have sickle cell anemia and others only carry the disease, that is, they can pass on the disease to their children without having it themselves.

2d(2)   Comparison and Contrast

Uses: to show how two people, places, or things are alike or different in order to describe either one more fully.

How to use it: in the topic sentence make clear how you are comparing the two things. Do not try to compare the things in too many ways. Make sure to complete all the contrasts promised. Make sure to compare the things in a point-by-point manner and not just write a few things about one and a few different, unrelated things about the other.

> Books obviously have distinctive characteristics that set them apart from other media. Certainly, they differ from other print media, such as newspapers and magazines, in that they are bound and covered and are consecutive from beginning to end. Because books often take a year or more to produce, they are less timely than newspapers and magazines. Nevertheless, like other mass media, they are produced by professional communicators and generally distributed to relatively large and diverse audiences. One obvious difference from several other media is that, like movies, they are not basically supported by advertising (although some publishers are experimenting with this idea). Thus, books have to earn profits for their producers on the basis of their content. More than other media, moreover, books are made to last, and their form lends itself to in-depth, durable exploration and development of a topic or idea.
>
> —Melvin DeFluer and Everette Dennis

2d(3)   Classification

Uses: to describe, to explain, to prove.

How to use it: in the topic sentence clearly break the subject up into parts. In the following sentences discuss each part separately and in detail, showing how the part relates to the main subject and how it is different from other aspects of the main subject.

> The most direct way to get a clear picture of changes in physical development during the years from two to five is to visit a nursery school and watch the children at play. Differences between two- and five-year-olds are apparent not only in physical size, but also in coordination of both small and large muscle activities. Most two-year-olds have a well-coordinated walk, but they run with difficulty. If they get on a tricycle, they may use only one pedal at a time. Great effort and concentration may be required to get food on a spoon, and spills at the dining table are common. When getting dressed, they may help by pushing their arms and legs into shirt sleeves and pants, but they cannot get into these garments by themselves. They negotiate stairs one step at a time, putting down first one foot and then the other before moving to the next step. Most five-year-olds, by contrast, can run easily and use play equipment with considerable skill. They can handle tricycles with proficiency and may also be able to ride a bicycle (with or without training wheels). They can handle spoons and forks well (although knives may still be a problem), and spills while eating are more likely to be due to carelessness than to lack of coordination.

They can dress themselves easily, although tying shoe laces may still be a problem. They can go up and down stairs by alternating feet and climb with agility.

—Robert F. Biehler and Lynne M. Hudson

2d(4)   Cause and Effect

Uses: to explain why something happens or what results from something else.

How to use it: in the topic sentence, state the effect whose *cause* or causes the paragraph will explore, or state an event or idea whose *results* the paragraph will explore.

It seems a deadly form of sex discrimination: When the National Weather Service tallies up the deaths caused by lightning each year in the United States, an overwhelming number of the victims are male. Of 74 lightning-related deaths in 1990, females numbered only seven. Little research has focused on the causes of the disparity. But it's acknowledged that men tend to be outdoors more than women, at work or at play, and are thus more vulnerable to a strike. Examining lightning fatalities from 1968 through 1985, the Centers for Disease Control found that 85 percent were male and that a third of them died on the job. The victims included farm laborers, construction workers, nurserymen, and a land surveyor. Since 1959 Florida has led the nation in lightning deaths and injuries. Apart from those killed at work, many are struck while fishing from boats, others while at the beach or on the golf course. "There's probably that old macho ego," says Roger Tanner, a weather researcher. "A male may not be cautious and take cover readily."

—*National Geographic*

2e   WRITING TRANSITIONS

Sentences relate to each other, so your writing should show the transitions, or connections, between them. Here are some ways in which you can show these links between sentences. (Also see **3f.**)

2e(1)   Repeating Important Words

A key idea of your paragraph may be expressed in a few words; repeating these key words throughout your paragraph will remind the reader of your main idea. Be careful not to repeat words that are not key words, because then they will seem more important than they actually are.

2e(2)   Using Pronouns

Pronouns (see Chapter 8) take the place of the actual names of places, people, or things. Once you have named a person, place, or thing, you can automatically refer back to him, her, or it by using a pronoun. The pronoun reminds the reader that you are still talking about the same subject. Make sure that the word the pronoun refers to is always clear, and that you use the correct form of the pronoun.

2e(3)   Repeating Sentence Patterns

By using the same sentence pattern over and over, writers can sometimes add details and specifics in a dramatic way. In Martin Luther King, Jr.'s famous "I Have a Dream" speech, for example, sentence after sentence begins with the phrase *I have a dream that* . . . The rhythm of this pattern does much to make the speech powerful. Of course, you do not want to overuse a sentence pattern.

2e(4)   Using Words of Transition

Words of transition show how two ideas or statements are related to each other. For example, the word *later* lets you know that the second thing happened after the first; the word *therefore* shows that the first thing is the cause of the second. Words of transition are especially important when there are many parts to your topic idea and each of the parts has a special relationship to the others.

The following paragraph, for example, uses transitional words (as well as pronouns and repeated words) to create a logical argument.

> *When* social scientists discuss what makes people become criminals, they usually consider either of two factors. The *first* factor is social circumstances, the difficult conditions that drive or entice people into crime. The *second* factor is genetic inheritance, biological characteristics that may define criminal personalities. *However, this* either/or thinking may be a problem, according to two Harvard researchers. *Instead,* they argue, researchers should look at the interaction of the two factors. *As a result,* we will begin to understand how biological traits are channeled by social circumstances to produce criminals.

Without the transitional words, the paragraph would break apart into a series of disjointed statements: "Social scientists discuss things. People

WORDS OF TRANSITION

Purpose	Transitional Words
To add	*also, and, and then, too, plus, in addition, furthermore, moreover, again, on top of that, another, first, second, third, . . .*
To put in time order	*now, then, before, after, afterward, earlier, later, immediately, soon, next, in a few days, meanwhile, gradually, suddenly, finally, previously*
To put in space order	*near, near to, far, far from, in front of, beside, in the rear of, beyond, above, below, to the right, to the left, around, surrounding, on one side, inside, outside, alongside*
To compare	*in the same way, similarly, just like, just as, likewise*
To contrast	*but, still, however, on the other hand, on the contrary, yet, nevertheless, despite, in spite of, even though, in contrast, instead*
To show cause and effect	*because, since, so, consequently, as a result, therefore, then, accordingly, hence, thus*
To show purpose	*for this reason, for this purpose, so that this may happen*
To emphasize	*indeed, in fact, surely, necessarily, certainly, without any doubt, in any event, truly, again, to repeat*
To give examples	*for example, for instance, as an illustration, specifically, to be specific, as proof*
To summarize	*in summary, in conclusion, as I have shown, as has been stated, in other words, in brief, to sum up, thus, so*

become criminals. Social circumstances are a factor." The table on page 28 lists words and phrases of transition. Keep it handy when you are writing something complex.

2f   ENDING THE PARAGRAPH

The last sentence of a paragraph should mark the end of your thoughts on the topic. A quick summary, especially if it has a clever turn, often makes a strong ending sentence. For example, one student ended a paragraph about the problem of getting to a boring eight o'clock class, "So you can see, I get up from a good sleep at six o'clock in the morning, just so I can fight my way on the subway to get to a class where I sleep again."

Sometimes a topic has a natural end; the last detail completes the picture while reminding the reader of the main idea of the paragraph. One student used this method to end her description of a boring class, "As I escape that horrible classroom, I hear my friends' voices down the hallway and my heart leaps in delight."

Another method is to come to a conclusion, to decide what all the details in the paragraph really mean. For instance, a third student responded to a boring class by being absent and not doing the work. He ended a paragraph describing his sorry fate in this way: "Things are getting so bad that, even though I need the credits, I will have to drop that awful course." (The list of suggestions for ending an essay on page 37 may give you more ideas for single-sentence paragraph endings.)

3

The Essay

An **essay** develops one main thought, using a number of paragraphs. The structure of an essay is much like that of a paragraph, as the following list shows:

A paragraph has	*An essay has*
One main idea developed in a number of sentences	One main idea developed in a number of paragraphs
A topic sentence	An opening paragraph with a topic statement
Middle sentences giving supporting details, explanation, description, and so forth	Middle paragraphs giving supporting details, explanation, description, and so forth
A strong ending sentence	A strong ending paragraph
An orderly paragraph pattern	An orderly plan or outline

The suggestions in Chapter 2 on how to write a good paragraph should help you write a good essay. And, of course, everything you learned in Chapter 1 applies here, too.

However, because an essay is longer and more complex than a paragraph, you must be more thoughtful, more organized, and more aware of the choices you make.

Steps in Writing an Essay

▶ Decide what you are going to write about (see **1a**).
▶ Discover and arrange the details you need (see **2b, 2c,** and **3a**).
▶ Bring the essay topic into focus in one sentence (see **3b**).

▶ Write a partial or full outline (see **3c**).
▶ Use the outline to write the essay (see **3c**).
▶ Make the topic clear and interesting in the opening paragraph (see **3d**).
▶ Develop the topic in the middle paragraphs (see **3e**).
▶ Let the reader know how the essay fits together (see **3f**).
▶ Close the essay with a strong last paragraph (see **3g**).
▶ Hand in the best work you can do (see **1d**).

3a DETAILS AND THEIR ARRANGEMENT

Since you need more supporting details for an essay than for a paragraph, you need a plan to discover the kinds of details you want and to keep the details in order. Otherwise, you will be lost in a maze of details that have no pattern. You will have no way to know what you need. Start by jotting down a few details. Soon you will find that they fall into clearly marked groups. For example, if you are describing a friend, some details will be about looks, some about personality, and some about achievements. These groups of details will often match the topics you will later choose for the separate paragraphs of the essay. You can now look over the groups to see if there are any other important details that need to be added. You can also see whether you need more details in any group.

3b THE TOPIC STATEMENT

Just as each paragraph usually needs a topic sentence, each essay needs a **topic statement.** After you have gathered details and thought about the topic, you should state clearly in one sentence the main point of the essay.

When you finally write the essay, you will probably use this sentence, or one like it, as the last sentence of the opening paragraph. Once you have written the topic statement for the essay, you will be able to judge whether you need to gather any more details or to develop any more ideas to cover your topic completely.

3c   THE OUTLINE

The topic statement and the groups of details should provide a partial outline or plan for the essay. Whether or not you need a full outline depends on how complex your essay will be and how well you know what you want to say. If you have a good idea of what you will write about, then you probably don't need a full outline. If, on the other hand, you still do not have the essay in focus, you should make an outline. Sometimes a quick sketch of an outline will be enough, but sometimes you may need a full, detailed outline, particularly if the essay will be long or complex.

If you cannot write an outline before you write a first draft, you may find it helpful to write an outline *after* the first draft. In this way you can see whether your writing is logical and clear. Although some people find it difficult to follow an outline as they write, everyone can use an outline as a check on what has already been written.

An outline is a detailed plan of an essay. All ideas and details are organized in main headings and subheadings. Whenever any heading has two or more parts, you break it up into subheadings. The most important ideas are numbered with Roman numerals (I, II, III, IV, . . .) and start at the left margin. Supporting ideas and details are indented and numbered with capital letters (A, B, C, D, . . .), numbers (1, 2, 3, 4, . . .), and small letters (a, b, c, d, . . .) in order of subordination. An outline looks like this:

Title

I. First main idea
   A. Supporting idea
      1. Detail
      2. Detail
      3. Detail
         a. Minor detail
         b. Minor detail
   B. Supporting idea
      1. Detail
      2. Detail
   C. Supporting idea
II. Second main idea

To create an outline that will be the most helpful to you as you write, make sure that

▶ only main ideas form main headings.
▶ all the subheadings relate to the main headings under which they appear.
▶ all the headings in a series are of the same type.
▶ all the headings are clearly different so that they don't overlap. (If there is too much overlapping, you must reorganize the information.)
▶ whenever you break down a heading, you have at least two subheadings.
▶ everything important that appears in the essay is included.
▶ all the items are indented correctly.
▶ you put a period after each letter or number.

The most complete kind of outline is the sentence outline. Each item in the outline is expressed as a complete sentence. You may make a less complete topic outline by using only short groups of words. With a sketch outline you only briefly note the main ideas for each of the main parts of the essay.

3c(1)   The Sketch Outline

Here is a sketch outline for the sample essay "Growing Up with Computers" on pages 37–39.

Growing Up with Computers

I. Intro—growing computer use and effect on me
II. first effect—on hand-eye coordination
III. problem solving
IV. interacting with the computer's mind and the programmer's mind
V. extending your mind
VI. thinking like a computer and thinking with a computer

3c(2)   The Topic Outline

Here is a topic outline for the first three paragraphs of the sample essay "Growing Up with Computers" on pages 37–39. Compare it with the sketch outline above.

Growing Up with Computers

I. Growing computer use in my life
  A. Video games in first grade
  B. Mother's PC
    1. Brought home in fourth grade
    2. Took over
    3. Weekend hacking
  C. School
    1. Appearance in classrooms
    2. High school computer courses
  D. First generation to grow up on computers
  E. Impact
II. Effect on hand-eye coordination
  A. Quick response for playing games
  B. Other skills neglected
    1. Ball playing
    2. Delicate construction
III. Effect on problem solving
  A. Constant problem solving
  B. Computers as complex multiple environments
    1. Finding way through
    2. Figuring out how programs work
    3. Figuring out how to make programs work
    4. Making my own programs

3c(3)   The Sentence Outline

Here is a sentence outline for the first three paragraphs of the sample essay "Growing Up with Computers" on pages 37–39. Compare it with the sketch and topic outlines above.

Growing Up with Computers

I. I have been using computers since an early age.
  A. I got my first video game in first grade.
  B. When my mother brought home a PC, I soon took it over and started hacking.
  C. Computers also started appearing in school classrooms, and classes were devoted to the computer in high school.
  D. I was part of the first generation to grow up on computers, and computers have had a big impact on me.
II. Using computers has affected my hand-eye coordination.
  A. Playing computer games quickened my response to visual stimuli as I shot down invaders from space.
  B. However, I had little time to develop other hand-eye skills needed for ball playing or constructing models.

III. Using computers has developed my problem-solving skills.
   A. Using computers requires constant problem solving.
   B. Computers contain complex worlds that you must find your way through.
   C. You need to solve problems to make programs work and to design your own programs.

3d   THE OPENING PARAGRAPH

The opening paragraph of an essay should state the topic of the essay, show the interest or importance of the topic, and get the essay moving. In the opening paragraph you want to let the reader know where the essay is going, and you want to start getting it there. The opening should be short and effective: give the basic facts, get the reader involved, and move on to the middle paragraphs or body of the essay. Use the topic statement—you should rewrite it to fit the paragraph—as the last sentence of the opening paragraph to point out the exact purpose of the essay.

Hints for Writing Opening Paragraphs

▶ Explain or describe the main topic.
▶ Give background information.
▶ Tell a story that illustrates the main point of the essay.
▶ Ask a question that the essay will answer.
▶ Describe an effect if the essay will explain its cause.
▶ Start with the most exciting or dramatic moment in a story.
▶ Give a striking fact, odd problem, or interesting sidelight that is related to the essay topic.
▶ Use a vivid quotation from a good source.

3e   THE MIDDLE PARAGRAPHS

The middle paragraphs examine each part of the topic in detail. Basically, each part of the topic should be in a separate paragraph. Each paragraph should have a topic sentence that shows the main point of the paragraph and how that point relates to the essay topic. Each middle paragraph should develop its topic sentence according to some clear pattern, either time order, space order, order of importance, or any of the other patterns described in **2c** and **2d**.

The middle paragraphs must also relate to each other. There must be some reason why the third paragraph comes after the second and before the fourth. For example, if each paragraph of an essay describes one step in the legal battle to allow girls to play Little League baseball, you will probably place the paragraphs in time order. If you are explaining how to grow vegetables, you probably will put the paragraphs on soil and weather conditions before the paragraph on planting.

3f   TRANSITIONS

You remember that transitions help fit the parts of your writing together by making connections between sentences and paragraphs. You can tie the paragraphs of an essay together in several different ways.

▶   Repeat important words or phrases: see **2e(1).**
▶   Use pronouns to refer back to an important person, place, or thing: see **2e(2).**
▶   Repeat sentence patterns: see **2e(3).**
▶   Begin a new paragraph by referring back to the main idea of the previous one: see **2e(4).** By using a word of transition and a word like *this,* you can relate the ideas of the new paragraph to an idea you developed earlier. For example, the following sentence might begin a middle paragraph in an essay called "What Happens When You Exercise":

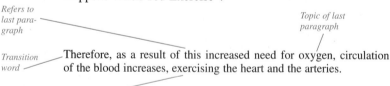

Refers to last paragraph   *Topic of last paragraph*

Transition word — Therefore, as a result of this increased need for oxygen, circulation of the blood increases, exercising the heart and the arteries.

Topic of new paragraph

3g   THE CONCLUSION

The last paragraph of an essay should, either directly or indirectly, show the reader that you have finished and remind him or her of the main point of the essay. Often a phrase of transition such as *in short, so we can see,* or *finally* will signal to the reader that you are now going to write a few sentences that sum up or reflect the whole essay. If your essay is complex and you feel the reader could use a reminder of all your points, you could end with a summary. However, there are other, more graceful ways to end.

Hints for Writing Conclusions

▶ Summarize the main points.

▶ State your conclusions, discoveries, or theories based on the facts of the essay.

▶ Discuss the effects of the facts and ideas of the essay.

▶ Point out new questions your essay raises.

▶ Suggest a solution of the problems you have discussed.

▶ Quote someone who supports your main point.

▶ Refer to the beginning of the essay.

▶ Apply the idea of your essay to some other area of importance.

3h A SAMPLE ESSAY

As you read the sample essay on the following pages, look at the comments in the margin, which will help you review the points discussed in this chapter.

Growing Up with Computers

Opening paragraph

Back-ground facts

Transi-tional time words sig-nal se-quence

Conclu-sion of se-quence

Topic statement of essay

Transition signals first point

Topic sen-tence of second paragraph

A dozen years ago, when I was in first grade, my dad brought our first video game home. When I was in fourth grade, my mother brought home a personal computer from the office. I soon nagged her into letting me use it and within a year I had taken it over and spent my weekends hacking. Computers started appearing in classrooms and by high school you could take a menu of computer-based courses. I was in the first generation that grew up with computers. And computers have had a major impact on how I have grown up.

The most obvious effect has been my hand-eye coordination. With small motions of my hand I have learned to shoot down increasingly clever, quick, and

Qualifica-
tion

numerous creatures from outer space. This does not
mean I can catch a ball or construct delicate wooden
models. Having spent so much time clicking buttons in

Return to
main
point

front of a video screen, I have had little time to develop
those other hand-eye skills. But I am ready to fight an
electronic war and throw up an electronic shield to

Transition
signals
order of
importance

protect my virtual reality.

A bit more importantly, working with computers

Topic sen-
tence of
third
paragraph

has taught my mind to be constantly solving problems.
Although computers may look like plastic boxes, they are
rich universes containing multiple worlds that you have
to find your way through. I have had to figure out how

Supporting
details

each new game or program works. I have also had to
figure out, when it doesn't work, if there is some way I
can make it work. Eventually I started to figure out how
to make my own programs and games that I think work
even better.

Transition
refers to
previous
paragraph
but moves
argument
to a new
level

In solving problems with a computer you are
interacting with other minds. In one sense you are
interacting with the mind of a computer. You have to
learn to think how a computer thinks—how it organizes

Topic sen-
tence of
fourth
paragraph

information and processes, how it works. If you figure
out how the computer thinks, you can work with it a lot

Transition
indicates
two levels
of this
para-
graph's
discussion

better. But in working with a program, you are also
interacting with the mind of another human being who
wrote the program. Each programmer has a certain way
of solving problems and setting up environments for you

Connects to beginning of paragraph but emphasizes order of increasing importance

to work with. You relate to the other person through the intermediary of the computer program. So even more than learning to solve problems, you learn about other minds.

Transition indicates last, but most important point

Topic sentence of fifth paragraph

Explanation

Move toward lighter conclusion

Finally, by learning to work with other minds, you learn to use the extensive power of the many minds and massive information stored within computers. You become much smarter, not because you own a smart machine, but because you learn how to use the machine's multiple intelligences to extend your own abilities. I have grown up to rely on the computer to help me with almost everything, from writing and mathematics to amusements to art. I haven't yet found a way to have it help me with my love life. Poor me. But perhaps I will figure that out too.

Conclusion returns to time-order family story of introduction

Contrast between generations emphasizes main point of essay

Reference back to processes discussed in essay

Summary of overall effect of using the computer

My parents say I have become too smart for them. Most of their work now gets done on the computer, and every time they have a new program or a new project to work out, they let me explain it to them. They are smart people, but although they use computers all the time, they did not grow up with computers. So they just do not know how to think like a computer and even more how to think with a computer. They just use it. I and my friends have made the computer part of ourselves. So maybe we are smarter by a couple of microchips.

4

Writing from Sources

In college much of your writing is directly related to course reading. You write essays based on material in your textbooks. You write responses to articles and books you have been assigned to read. You synthesize information from several sources you have found in library research or research on the Internet. You write analyses of various texts you read. You write original arguments using information you have gathered. Learning how to draw on the words of others, how to think about and critically evaluate those words, and then how to react to them with your own thoughts and information are all central to the college experience.

In writing about what others have written, you need to identify their ideas and information accurately, so that your own responses and criticisms will be based on a good understanding of those writers' statements. This is where the skills of **summary writing** enter in (see **4a**).

In college it usually isn't enough to repeat the information and ideas of others: you must then go on to develop your own perspectives and thoughts. Several types of essay writing help you build on and respond to the writings of others so as to develop your own point of view: the **response essay** (see **4b**); the **synthesis essay** (see **4c**); and the **original argument using sources** (see **4d**).

When using sources, it is important for you to document exactly what you have taken from them. Attempting to pass off other people's writing, ideas, and information as your own is **plagiarism** (see **4e**). The way to avoid plagiarism is to **document your sources** (see **4f**) and make an accurate **Works Cited list** (see **4g**).

4a   SUMMARY WRITING

A summary is a shortened version of a passage or article. A summary restates the most important ideas and information of the original piece of writing. Depending on the purpose of the summary and the length of the original, the summary may be as long as 25 percent of the length of the original or as short as 1 percent. Writing summaries is useful as a study aid, to help yourself identify and remember information and ideas from textbooks and other readings. Exam questions, as well, often ask you to do little more than summarize some of the material you have read. On the other hand, a simple summary will not be adequate for most essay questions on exams or for other essay assignments. Since college teachers usually expect more than just a restatement of textbook materials, you need to become aware of the distinction between summary writing and other forms of writing using sources, forms such as the response essay, the synthesis essay, and the original argument.

In writing a summary you do not add your own thoughts (which you can write in a response essay or your journal); all the material in the summary comes from your source text. Because you are taking all that material from it, you need to identify the source in a heading or a tag line, to make clear that the only work you are adding is the work of summarizing.

Steps to Writing Effective Summaries

▶ *Read* the entire passage for full understanding.
▶ *Identify the gist* or main idea of each paragraph or section.
▶ *Write the gist* down in a phrase or sentence.
▶ *Select the major points* or major details. You may wish to highlight, underline, or circle those details you want to put into the summary, and draw a line through material that is less important, material you will not use in the summary.
▶ *Decide* which you are writing: a descriptive summary or an informative summary. A *descriptive summary* is in your own voice, describing the passage (e.g., "The first section of this article begins by presenting three reasons why we should be concerned about global warming . . ."). An *informative summary* presents the information directly, as in the original (e.g., "Global warming should concern us for three reasons . . .").
▶ *Organize* the material you have selected, so as to reflect the sense of the original.
▶ *Rewrite* the gist statement and the selected points and details in coherent prose that ties the whole sense of the piece together.
▶ *Identify the source* of the material summarized—use either a heading or a tag line at the end.

4b   THE RESPONSE ESSAY

In a **response essay** you develop one of your own thoughts in reaction to what you have read. The reaction may be based on your own experience, on your own line of reasoning, or on other things you have learned and read. In this essay your voice needs to take over, making it just like any other essay you might write about your ideas, knowledge, or experience, except that you must first tie it into the corresponding passage from your reading. In the opening paragraph, you should explain the specific idea you are responding to and give the source, using appropriate documentation techniques (see **4f** and **4g**). The topic sentence (**3b**) should then indicate your main reaction or response. The remainder of the essay should be organized and developed just as any other essay you would write, following the guidelines in Chapter 3 and in this chapter. Teachers will often assign response essays to learn what you think about the material you are reading or what kinds of connections you can make to your own life. Response essays connecting concepts from reading to your personal experience or social surroundings are especially common in social sciences classes where teachers want you to see how the specialized concepts you are learning apply to actual life.

Sample Opening for a Response

Nicholas Backlund reports that many companies have adopted environmentally aware policies, from McDonald's use of recycled packaging material to Ben and Jerry's production of "Rain Forest Crunch" ice cream, whose profits are contributed to saving the Amazon jungle. This seems an important trend, because it shows major companies affirming that good ecology is good business. Too often we hear companies saying, We would really like to help protect the environment, but we are in business to make money. If we worried about every good cause, we would go broke. But now a number of highly profitable companies are showing that this just isn't so.

While working last summer in a fast-food
restaurant I saw an enormous amount of waste that had
nothing to do with profits or efficiency. For example . . .

Source Cited
Backlund, Nicholas. "Corporate Consciences."
International Design December 1990: 40-43.

4c   THE SYNTHESIS ESSAY

In a **synthesis essay** you must tie together the information, details,
and ideas from several sources to present an overall coherent description
of some event, idea, or other topic. You must do more than simply
string together summaries of the different sources. Instead you must
show how all the parts connect into a single picture. In your opening
paragraph, after you introduce the subject, give as a topic sentence a statement of the overall picture your subject presents. The following paragraphs
should develop that picture in an orderly way, following the connections
among the source materials. To tie your writing together, pay special
attention to transitions (see **2e**), and remember to thoroughly document
any information that comes from your sources (see **4f** and **4g**). Teachers
in the humanities and social sciences frequently assign synthesis essays to
help you gain information through research and draw your research together
into a meaningful picture.

Sample Opening for a Synthesis

Recent articles in design journals show an
increasing awareness of environmental concerns on the
part of industrial designers and describe creative
attempts to redesign products to be more ecologically
sound. Approaches are concerned with packaging and
products. The trend now is to minimize packaging, to
make it out of ecologically sound materials, and to
increase recyclability (Erlhoff 6; Aldersley and Williams

44). Products are also being redesigned with a new concern for materials as well as with a concern for what will happen to the products once they have reached the end of their usable lives (Tompkins 12).

Suggestions for minimizing packaging have ranged from asking how much packaging is really necessary (Forest and Viemeister 15) to calls to eliminate packaging altogether (Kaldjian 18). According to Forest and Viemeister, packaging creates one-third the weight and one-half the volume of our current garbage . . .

Sources Cited

Aldersley, Hugh, and Dorsey Williams. "The Green Imperative." International Design December 1990: 44-47.

Erlhoff, Michael. "Design and Ecology." Innovation Summer 1990: 6-7.

Forest, Ann De, and Tucker Viemeister. "Waste Not, Want Not." International Design December 1989: 64-67.

Kaldjian, Paul. "Environmental Results Through Industrial Design." Innovation Summer 1990: 15-19.

Tompkins, David. "'Plastic Is Bad' and other myths." Innovation Summer 1990: 11-14.

4d THE ORIGINAL ARGUMENT USING SOURCES

In the **original argument using sources** you go beyond the synthesis to develop conclusions, evaluations, or knowledgeable opinions on the basis of your research. In the introduction, as in any opinion essay, you identify the importance of the subject and then state in the topic sentence the position you will take on the subject. Each of the following paragraphs then develops the points of your argument or the details backing up your conclusions or evaluations. The details of your research—what you have learned from your reading—simply fill out and support the argument you are making. Again, of course, you must completely document all the material you take from the sources, but the overall voice and point of view of the essay should remain your own. The argument using sources is the most common writing assignment made by college teachers, and is often called a term paper or research paper. Many students, not realizing that a term paper asks for an original argument, provide only a synthesis essay or, even worse, a loosely connected series of summaries of different sources.

Sample Opening for an Original Argument Using Sources

The industrial design industry has been showing increasing awareness of the environment, and has proposed many changes for redesigning packaging and products to help preserve our environment. These efforts aimed at reducing packaging and making packaging recyclable, while worth praise, barely make a dent in the amount of trash and pollution we produce every day. One way to decrease the overall waste and pollutants would be to change our patterns of consumption and learn to live with less, as many environmentalists have argued. But do you really expect people who have tasted plenty to want to live with less? What we need to do is understand what consumers desire in the modern world and see if there is a way to satisfy those desires more efficiently and with fewer material resources that need to be used, transformed, and transported. That will provide a real challenge for product designers.

The movement toward more ecologically sound packaging is only a few years old, but many companies are now paying attention to it, at least for publicity value

(Backlund 42). However, most of the concern has been about plastics, which comprise less than one-twelfth of our landfill trash (Tompkins 11). If we want to reduce the great amount of pollution that is cluttering up the world, we must first ask, where does the great majority of pollution and waste come from . . .

Sources Cited

Backlund, Nicholas. "Corporate Consciences." International Design December 1990: 40-43.
Tompkins, David "'Plastic Is Bad' and other myths." Innovation Summer 1990: 11-14.

4e   PLAGIARISM

Plagiarism is the misdeed of passing off someone else's work as your own. In the commercial world of books, movies, and songs, the words people write and the ideas they create are valuable properties that may be worth many dollars. In college the value is in your learning, thinking, and problem solving. The distrust created by passing off others' work as your own interferes with learning, with developing your own thoughts and ideas, and with the easy communication that is crucial to education. The success of education depends to a considerable extent on a trusting relationship between teachers and students. Although plagiarism, if detected, can sometimes lead to severe punishments, even to expulsion, there is *always* a high educational cost for plagiarism, even if the plagiarist is never caught.

Sometimes plagiarism arises from a misunderstanding as to exactly what material needs to be credited. If your class is using just one textbook and the teacher asks you an exam question about factual material from it, of course he or she assumes that you will rely on material from the textbook, which in this situation does not need to be credited explicitly. However, once the situation gets more complex—if, for example, the class is assigned two or more books, or you need to find sources at the library, or you make use of any additional information from your own reading—you must give credit to your sources, following the procedures described in **4f** and **4g**.

Sometimes plagiarism arises from not understanding which aspects of borrowed materials must be given credit. If you use someone else's words, even just a two- or three-word phrase, you must enclose those words in quotation marks to indicate that they *are* someone else's words, and you must also document the source. If you do not use someone else's exact words but do use his or her ideas or information, you must document the source. The only exception is when you are using common knowledge—facts that most people aware of a general subject area know about and that appear in multiple sources.

Sometimes plagiarism arises from students' forgetting to keep good records. In taking notes, it is important to identify the source from which you are taking them and to indicate when you are using exact wording from your source. It is also important to distinguish your own thoughts from the material you are taking from your sources. In this way, when you use your notes later to write an essay, you will know which material you need to document and which you can present as your own.

Sometimes, out of panic, students may intentionally plagiarize. When a student feels overwhelmed by a subject or has not left enough time for completing assignments, he or she may be tempted to copy materials from other sources without giving credit. However, it is rare to find a student who will intentionally cheat by plagiarism if an honorable alternative seems available. The alternative is to get help before panic sets in: explain your problem or your confusion to the teacher while there is still time to complete the assignment. Even if panic has already set in and little time remains, if you present your problem to the teacher, he or she may be more flexible and helpful than you imagine. Any teacher would prefer you to do your own best work (no matter how inadequate you may feel) or to turn in an assignment late than for you to pretend that someone else's work is your own.

4f DOCUMENTING SOURCES

Every time you use a quotation, information, or an idea from a book, magazine, or other printed source, you must state where you got the quotation, information, or idea. Even if you paraphrase (change the wording) or summarize (write in brief form) the material in your own words, you must give credit to the source. Quotations must accurately follow the exact wording of the original, and be identified by quotation marks or indentation (see **13a** and **13b**).

You may document your sources using any of a number of different styles, depending on your academic discipline and the preferences of your instructor. Styles of documentation all provide much the same information but differ in format. For the sake of consistency and ease of reference, you should follow precisely the style required by the teacher, profession, or journal for which you are writing. If you don't know what documentation style is required, simply ask. Disciplines in the humanities typically use the Modern Language Association (MLA) style, the social sciences use the American Psychological Association (APA) style, and the sciences use the Council of Biology Editors (CBE) and the American Chemical Society (ACS) styles. Each of these organizations publishes handbooks specifying the details of documentation formats.

This chapter presents the documentation style required by the Modern Language Association (MLA). According to the MLA, you no longer need to use footnotes to document sources. Instead, you should give a **Works Cited** list at the end of your paper. In your paper, whenever you use information, an idea, or a quotation from a work, you refer to that list.

You refer to the Works Cited lists by giving the author's last name and the page number of the work from which you got the material. You can give the name and page number in the sentence itself or in parentheses.

For example, you could refer to material taken from page 32 of the book *Great Scientific Experiments* by Rom Harre in any one of the following ways:

"Aristotle must surely be ranked as among the greatest biologists" (Harre 32).

Harre comments, "Aristotle must surely be ranked as among the greatest biologists" (32).

Harre believes that Aristotle is a top biologist (32).

If you have more than one book by Harre in your Works Cited list, include a short version of the title of the book you are referring to.

(Harre, Great Experiments 32)

4g   WORKS CITED LIST

The information you must include in your Works Cited list comes from the title and copyright pages of the books you use. If you quote from a magazine article, you will need to look at the first page of the article and the masthead of the magazine. The masthead, which lists publication information, usually appears near the front of the magazine, close to the table of contents.

Here is the basic form for Works Cited listings, showing the elements you must provide, in proper order, for books and articles. Note the style of punctuation.

Book	Author. Title. City of Publication: Publisher, year.
Article	Author. "Article Title." Magazine Title Volume number (Date): inclusive pages.
Electronic document	Author. "Title." Electronic site. Online. Date Accessed. Electronic Address.

Arrange the items in the list in alphabetical order according to the author's last name. If there is more than one author, the second and third authors should be given first name first. If there is no author, begin with the title.

Sample Items for Works Cited List

Books:

One author	Harre, Rom. Great Scientific Experiments. Oxford: Phaidon, 1981.
Two authors	Glazer, Nathan, and Daniel Patrick Moynihan. Beyond the Melting Pot. Cambridge, Mass.: M.I.T. Press, 1963.
Editor	Kramer, Samuel Noah, ed. Mythologies of the Ancient World. Garden City, N.Y.: Doubleday, 1961.
Essay in a collection	Anthes, Rudolf. "Mythology in Ancient Egypt." Mythologies of the Ancient World. Ed. Samuel Noah Kramer. Garden City, N.Y.: Doubleday, 1961. 15-92.
Encyclopedia article	Kerr, K. Austin. "Lindbergh, Charles A." Academic American Encyclopedia. 1984 ed.

Magazine articles:

Signed	Shapiro, Laura. "Completely Adulterated Seafood." Newsweek 23 Feb. 1987: 64-65.

Unsigned   "Top Dog." Newsweek 23 Feb. 1987: 68.

Scholarly journal   Hashimoto, Irwin. "The Myth of the Attention-Getting Opening." Written Communication 3.1 (1986): 123-132. [3.1 means the first issue of volume 3]

Magazines published weekly (like *Newsweek*) or monthly often do not have volume and issue numbers. Notice, in the examples above, how the dates are treated.

Electronic documents:

Article in an electronic journal   Krause, Tom. "Mapping ECash: Eusing the Internet for Business Writing." Kairos 1.1. (8 November 1996): Online. Available: <http://english.ttu.edu/Kairos/1.1/features/Krause/ecash.html>

Comment on e-mail discussion list   Patrick Clauss. "'I think' and 'I feel'?" H-Net History of Rhetoric Discussion list. Online. 13 November 1996. <H-RHETOR@MSU.EDU>

Print material republished on the World Wide Web   Aristotle. Rhetoric. Trans. W. Rhys Roberts. New York: Modern Library, 1954. Online. The English Server at CMU. 8 November 1996. Available: <http://english-www.hss.cmu.edu/philosophy/aristotle/rhetoric:txt>

5

Logic

Logic, or correct reasoning, is important in clear writing. If you want readers to understand and be persuaded of your ideas, you should follow the principles below.

▶ *State the main point and stick to it.*

1. Don't jump around from one idea to another.

POOR | Crime is a big problem today. People also have problems in their love lives.
BETTER | The number of murders committed by young people has increased greatly this past year in New York City.

2. Don't try to make too many points at one time.

POOR | Family problems are caused by economic, social, psychological, educational, and accidental factors. I will discuss them all.
BETTER | Tensions sometimes occur in families because the children are better educated than their parents.

3. Don't get lost in side issues.

POOR | Several Asian societies have rapidly developing economies. It is difficult to predict how fast an economy will grow. Economics still requires guesswork.
BETTER | The rapidly developing economies of several Asian societies have presented challenges to the United States. Japan's rise as a modern economic power is being followed by South Korea, Taiwan, Malaysia, and Singapore. All of these countries are producing goods in competition with the United States.

4. Don't switch the topic to avoid discussing the main point.

POOR	Before I answer the charge that I took bribes, I will first ask my accusers what they have done for the people of this state.
BETTER	I have never taken bribes. To prove this, I place before you my complete financial records.

▶ *Back up all statements.*

1. Don't keep repeating the point without giving any proof or explanation.

POOR	Sincerity is the most important quality in a person. If a person is sincere, he or she must be good, because sincerity is so important.
BETTER	Sincerity often makes a person easier to talk to. My brother, for example, will never make up a big story or a sermon; he'll just tell me what he thinks. I can tell him my problems and get a straight answer.

2. Don't make broad, catch-all statements with little support.

POOR	These days everything is going downhill; politics, schools, people, businesses are all getting rottener every day.
BETTER	Some broadcast organizations have used deregulation as an excuse to decrease news coverage. According to figures gathered by the Federal Communications Commission . . .

3. Don't use words or phrases that assume your readers must agree with you—for example, *of course, certainly,* or *obviously*—to avoid developing detailed arguments and offering specific evidence for your ideas.

POOR	Of course, we all know the economy has been strong this year.
BETTER	In this past year, wholesale sales have risen 2.4 percent, retail sales have increased 2.8 percent, and the gross national product is up over 3.5 percent. These are the largest increases in the last decade, indicating a strong economy.

► *Pick good facts and be fair with them.*

1. Check all facts to make sure they are right.

POOR	Death Valley must be the driest spot on earth.
BETTER	Death Valley is very dry, but the Atacama Desert in Chile is so dry that the rainfall can barely be measured.

2. Make sure the facts come from a reliable source.

POOR	My uncle, Fred Bigmouth, told me that back in 1800 there weren't more than a few thousand people in the U.S.
BETTER	The United States Bureau of the Census reported that in 1800 there were 5,308,000 people in the nation.

3. Don't leave out facts just because they don't agree with what you are saying.

POOR	This college is really hard on us, making us do all this work.
BETTER	We do have a lot of schoolwork, but most teachers pace the assignments so that we won't have too much to do at any one time.

4. Don't slant or distort the facts.

POOR	Are you aware that the government is going to tear down this entire neighborhood to build a sewage plant?
BETTER	The Sanitation Department may build a garage for garbage trucks on an empty lot in order to speed up garbage pickups in the neighborhood.

► *Don't jump to conclusions.*

1. Don't think that one fact proves a whole case.

POOR	The fact that Professor Hardgrade gave me an F on the paper proves he is going to fail me for the whole year.
BETTER	I must go to Professor Hardgrade's office to find out why I got an F.

2. Don't think that just because one thing happened before another, the first event caused the second.

POOR   Because I washed my car this morning, it rained this afternoon.

BETTER   Unfortunately this afternoon's rain made my freshly washed car dirty again.

3. Don't assume there are only two sides to a question, yes or no, right or wrong.

POOR   If John J. Jones is not for us, he must be against us.

BETTER   Since John J. Jones has said nothing about our cause, he may not be very interested. We should find out where he stands.

4. Don't oversimplify complicated problems.

POOR   The only way to have peace is to destroy our enemies.

BETTER   Peace is a complex matter of power, diplomacy, and understanding.

▶ *Avoid loaded arguments that try to convince a reader by fear, prejudice, or other emotions rather than by reason.*

1. Don't call an opponent names or attack an opponent because you don't like the company he or she keeps.

POOR   People who don't agree with me must be either nuts, perverts, or radicals. Anyway, they get all their ideas from their wacko friends.

BETTER   I am sure people who don't agree with me have their reasons, but I find their arguments unconvincing because . . .

2. Don't flatter your readers or appeal to their snobbery.

POOR   A discriminating buyer knows true quality. We are sure you will appreciate the quality of the 1998 Moneymobile—made for those who understand the finer things in life.

BETTER   The 1998 Moneymobile offers all the luxuries that make driving a pleasure: leather seats, computerized controls, fine handling and control, and power to burn up the road.

3. Don't try to trick your readers into trusting you.

POOR   You can trust me, because I'm Honest Sam, the
              used-car man. I'd never steer you wrong.
BETTER   After checking with the Better Business
              Bureau and friends who have bought used cars
              from me, you'll know you can trust a deal with
              Sam.

4. Don't make readers insecure and frightened by saying,
   "Everybody agrees with me," "That's the way our grand-
   parents did it," or "An important person says you should
   believe me."

POOR   I think you should go along with this plan because
              the President has told me that every other presi-
              dent has done the same thing. Besides, everybody
              else has already joined the team.
BETTER   After looking at the facts I think you'll want to go
              along with this plan; but if you still don't want to,
              nobody will hold it against you.

▶ *Recognize valid opposing views.*

1. Don't avoid recognizing that valid opposing views exist.

POOR   No right-thinking, decent person could deny
              that our children should not be exposed to such
              trash.
BETTER   While some people may believe that young chil-
              dren should be informed about pornography, I
              believe raising the issue with them too early causes
              more problems than it solves.

2. Don't attribute opposing views to bad motives.

POOR   The only reason why my opponents are raising the
              issue of campaign reform is that they are trying to
              cover up their own misdeeds.
BETTER   Election time is not the best time to raise issues of
              campaign reform, since almost all candidates are
              taking the most advantage of the existing system.
              After the election, however, we should consider
              campaign reform seriously.

3. Take opposing views seriously. Accept those parts of opposing views that you consider justified.

POOR   Anybody who opposes the death penalty just lacks common sense.

BETTER   While the desire to create a compassionate society might suggest that we abolish the death penalty, compassion must be built on a sense of justice. If people do not feel criminals are held accountable for their crimes, leniency will be seen as weakness and injustice rather than as compassion.

▶ *Be certain when you are certain, but when you are less than sure, don't fake it.*

POOR   In twenty years I'll be sitting on the porch of my country estate signing autographed copies of my latest hit record album.

BETTER   I hope some day to be a rich and famous recording star, but these things are hard to predict.

UNIT TWO

The Sentence

6

Sentence Form

6a THE BASIC SENTENCE

In English, words are put together in units called sentences. Sentences can range from simple statements of only a few words to complex messages made up of many parts. However, unless you write long combinations of words carefully and correctly, complicated sentences can be very confusing. In order to write clear, long sentences, you must first master basic, simple sentences. Simple and direct sentences can, in fact, express most of the things that you have to say.

The basic English sentence has a subject and a verb: that is, the sentence mentions some person, place, thing, or idea (the **subject**) and tells what that person, place, thing, or idea does (the **verb**).

Subject	Verb
Jerilyn	thinks.
Jerilyn	is thinking.
Jerilyn	should have thought.

Remember: verbs may be made up of more than one word: *is thinking* and *should have thought* are complete verbs.

Sometimes words must be added to the subject and verb to give more information about the action. If someone or something receives the action, we add a word or group of words called the **object.**

Subject	Verb	Object
Kai	considers	the options.

Some verbs need other words to complete their meaning.

Subject	Verb	Verb completer
Oranges	taste	sour.
Metals	are	conductors.

59

Finding Sentence Parts

▶ *Look for the verb first.* Find the word or words that show action. Then test the word: use *I, we, you, she, he,* or *it* in front of the word you've picked as a verb to see if it makes sense.

In the sentence *Kai considers the options,* the word *considers* shows action. Then you test it: "She considers." It sounds right. The word *considers* is the verb.

If you thought *options* was the verb, as soon as you tested it, you'd reject that idea. "I option?" "She options?" (See **7a** for more help on finding verbs.)

▶ *Look for the subject next.* Ask *who* or *what* is doing the action of the verb. For the sentence *Kai considers the options,* ask, "Who considers?" Kai considers. *Kai* is the subject. For the sentence *A truck roared,* ask, "What roared?" A truck roared. *Truck* is the subject.

▶ *Look for the object last.* The object receives the action of the verb. Ask *whom* or *what* after you say the verb. For the sentence *Kai considers the options,* ask, "Kai considers what?" The answer is the options. The object of the sentence is *options.*

▶ *Look for verb completers after certain verbs.* Words that complete the verb by describing or naming the subject often come after these verbs:

am	was	feel(s)
is	were	look(s)
are	will be	smell(s)
		seems(s)
		appear(s)
		taste(s)

Oranges taste *sour.*

Metals are *conductors.*

The word *sour* completes the verb *taste* by describing the subject, *oranges.* The word *conductors* completes the verb *are* by giving an additional name to the subject, *metals.*

The basic sentence pattern is:

Subject—Verb—Object or Verb Completer

We can add other words and phrases telling more about the subject, verb, object, and verb completer, but the basic pattern stays the same. Notice in the following examples that no matter how many words and phrases we add to give more information, the basic pattern remains the same:

Kai [**subject**], confronted with a decision about what to do this summer, *considers* [**verb**] the options of working, traveling, going to school, or just taking it easy.

Containing citric acid, an ingredient in all citrus fruits, even ripe *oranges* [**subject**] *taste* [**verb**] to some degree *sour* [**verb completer**], although not usually as sour as lemons or grapefruit.

6b SENTENCE FRAGMENTS

A fragment is a broken-off part. A sentence fragment is a broken-off part of a sentence.

A sentence fragment is missing words that would turn it into a complete sentence. Sometimes a fragment has a subject with no verb; sometimes it has a verb with no subject. Sometimes a fragment is only a group of describing words without either subject or verb. Sometimes a sentence fragment is simply a broken-off part of the sentence that came before, needing only to be attached where it belongs.

Finding Fragments

▶ Does the sentence have a subject? See **6b(3)**.
▶ Does the sentence have a verb? **See 6b(2)**.
▶ Is the verb complete or is it only *part* of a two- or three-word verb? See **6b(4)** and **6b(5)**.
▶ Does the verb need a completer or an object? See **6a**.
▶ Is there a word group that should be linked to another sentence? See **6b(6)**.

6b(1) Descriptive Word Groups as Fragments

The troubled mayor consulted Professor Kona. *An expert on community relations.*

Some days nothing can make me move. *On hot and sunny days.*

To correct: The descriptive words usually refer to a person, thing, or action in a nearby sentence. Attach the fragment to that sentence or write a new sentence that explains the idea fully.

The troubled mayor consulted Professor Kona, an expert on community relations.

Some days nothing can make me move. On hot and sunny days, *I lie on the beach lazily.*

6b(2)   No-Verb Fragments

A new shopping mall just opened. *Department stores, record shops, and shoe stores.*

To correct: Add a verb and any needed verb completers or attach the fragment to a sentence (you may have to add some words).

A new shopping mall just opened. Department stores, record shops, and shoe stores *are already crowded.*

A new shopping mall just opened *with* department stores, record shops, and shoe stores.

6b(3)   No-Subject Fragments

The drummers finished their song. *Looked up at the audience.*

To correct: Combine the fragment with a nearby sentence. You may have to add words to make the combination make sense.

The drummers finished their song *and* looked up at the audience.

Or you can make a new sentence by adding a subject to the fragment.

The drummers finished their song. *They* looked up at the audience.

6b(4)   The *to* Form of the Verb as a Fragment

The court decided to uphold the fair housing law. To change patterns of discrimination.

To correct: Putting the word *to* in front of a verb changes the verb into an infinitive (see **7c**). An infinitive cannot by itself be the main verb of a sentence. In our example, *to change* cannot be the main verb. Further, there is no subject in the fragment. You must add a subject and full verb to make this kind of fragment a complete sentence.

The court decided to uphold the fair housing law. *The judges wanted* to change patterns of discrimination.

Or you can add the fragment to a nearby sentence, as long as it makes sense. You may have to add joining words like *and* or *in order to*.

The court decided to uphold the fair housing law *in order to* change patterns of discrimination.

6b(5) The *ing* Form of the Verb as a Fragment

> The explosion took everyone by surprise. *Bricks flying everywhere.*

To correct: In this fragment the word ending in *ing* (*flying*) is not a verb—it is only part of a verb. But you can add a word such as *is, are, was,* or *were* to make the *ing* form into a verb. (See **7c.**)

> The explosion took everyone by surprise. Bricks *were flying* everywhere.

Or you can add the fragment to a nearby sentence, as long as it makes sense.

> The explosion took everyone by surprise, bricks flying everywhere.

6b(6) Dependent Word Groups as Fragments

> Holidays in my village include storytelling. *When old people tell tales of long ago.*
>
> *Because we slept late.* We missed the first story.
>
> We arrived in time to hear Ramón. *Who tells of adventure in a deep, mysterious voice.*

To correct: A dependent word group (dependent clause) has a subject and a verb (as in all the fragments above); however, to be used correctly, it must link onto another sentence. The words *when, because,* and *who* in the fragments must connect to complete sentences.

> Holidays in my village include storytelling, *when* old people tell tales of long ago.
>
> *Because* we slept late, we missed the first story.
>
> We arrived in time to hear Ramón, *who* tells of adventure in a deep, mysterious voice.

You could also correct this kind of fragment by leaving out the linking word. (You may have to add some other words to complete the sentence.)

> Holidays in my village include storytelling. Old people tell tales of long ago.
>
> We slept late. We missed the first story.
>
> We arrived in time to hear Ramón. *He* tells of adventure in a deep, mysterious voice.

See also **6c(3).**

6c   COMBINED SENTENCES

To improve your writing, you often need to put together sentences that have related ideas. Two or more simple sentences may be combined to show that the statements fit closely together. The way you combine the sentences shows their relationship.

Here are some ways to combine sentences:

▶   Join two complete sentences together with a semicolon. See **6c(1)**.
▶   Join sentences together equally with the linking words *and, but, or, nor, for, yet, so* (coordinating conjunctions). See **6c(2)**.
▶   Make one sentence a dependent word group (dependent or subordinate clause) by using a dependent linking word (subordinating conjunction). Join the dependent word group to another sentence (independent clause). See **6c(3)**.

Make sure you combine sentences only when you have a good reason; otherwise, you will make sentences that go on and on unnecessarily. Overcombined sentences are rambling and hard to follow, as in this example:

> The watch that I bought downtown when I went to visit my aunt who lives in Chicago has worked very well, and I use it all the time; in fact, I am wearing it right now, and I intend to wear it tonight at a formal dinner party, and I will wear it tomorrow on the beach because it is good-looking and sturdy.

A number of smaller sentences would express the same message much more clearly:

> I bought a watch when I visited my aunt, who lives in downtown Chicago. The watch works very well; it is good-looking and sturdy. I wear it all the time. I am wearing it now and will wear it tonight at a formal dinner party and tomorrow at the beach.

See the chart on pages 66–67 for an explanation of how to punctuate combined sentences.

6c(1)   Two Sentences Joined by a Semicolon (coordination)

When two statements are very closely related, a semicolon joins them effectively. Often the two sentences joined by a semicolon have similar sentence structure.

Kevin couldn't tell a cow from a hog; he had never been out of the city.

Vera sent her parents in Hong Kong the good news by letter; her sister Irene sent the news by telegram.

You may also use a semicolon to join a sentence to another sentence that starts with a special connecting word like *however, therefore, furthermore, for example, on the other hand, in fact.*

Marylou ate no popcorn; *however,* she loved gum.

Children cry easily; *for example,* Marylou screamed because she hated popcorn.

Remember: the semicolon may be used to join two complete sentences only if the ideas of the sentences are connected very closely.

6c(2) Two Sentences Joined by *and, but, or, nor, for, yet,* or *so* (coordination)

When you combine sentences in this way, each sentence is equally important. Be sure to use a comma after the first sentence and before the connecting word.

Anthony used to own a motorcycle, *but* he sold it to Rosemarie.

Remember, do not string too many sentences together using these linking words. It is better to keep the sentences separate unless you have a good reason for putting them together.

6c(1) and **6c(2)** explain **coordination.** In coordination, you put together ideas that have the same importance. In other words, you join sentences of equal strength and value.

6c(3) Two Sentences Joined by a Dependent Linking Word (subordination)

Unlike *and, but, or, nor, for, yet, so,* and the semicolon, some words join sentences together so that one sentence needs the other in order to make sense. The part that cannot now stand by itself is called a **dependent clause.** The part that can stand by itself is the **independent clause.** Look at this sentence.

I take care of the car *because* I own it.

The word group *because I own it* cannot be a complete sentence. It depends on the complete thought *I take care of the car* in order to make sense. The word *because* is a dependent linking word; it turns *I own it* into a dependent clause.

Dependent linking words (subordinating conjunctions) begin word groups that, though they contain a subject and a verb, need to be joined to a complete sentence. You should make sure that you do not have a sentence fragment whenever you use one of the linking words.

Dependent Linking Words

▶   To show when: *before, after, while, since, until, once, whenever, when, as long as, as soon as*

▶   To show where: *where, wherever*

▶   To show why: *as, because, in order that, so that, since*

▶   To show how: *how, if*

▶   To show under what condition: *although, though, if, unless, provided, in case, once*

▶   To tell more about someone: *who, whose, that, whom*

▶   To tell more about some place or thing: *which, whose, that*

Dependent word groups come at the beginning, in the middle, or at the end of the complete sentence. Look at the following examples.

Dependent word group at the beginning:

> *Unless you hand in the final assignment,* you will not pass.
>
> *If that instructor threatens me again,* I will speak to the dean.

Dependent word group in the middle:

> The dean, *who was always in hiding,* could not be found.

Dependent word group at the end:

> The instructor was strict *when she set the deadlines for assignments.*
>
> The student found out *that you can't beat the system.*

When you join ideas together so that one depends on another, the process is called **subordination.** In subordination an idea of less importance (the **dependent** section) is connected to a complete thought (the **independent** section), which has more importance.

- PUNCTUATING COMBINED SENTENCES -

▶ Two sentences joined by a semicolon:

[Full sentence]; [full sentence].

OR

[Full sentence];
$\begin{cases} \textit{however} \\ \textit{therefore} \\ \textit{thus} \\ \textit{for example} \\ \textit{in any case} \\ \text{etc.} \end{cases}$
, [full sentence].

▶ Two sentences joined by *and, but, or, nor, for, yet, so:*

[Full sentence],
$\begin{cases} \textit{and} \\ \textit{but} \\ \textit{or} \\ \textit{nor} \\ \textit{for} \\ \textit{yet} \\ \textit{so} \end{cases}$
[full sentence].

▶ Two sentences joined by a dependent linking word:

1. Dependent word group at the beginning:

$\begin{cases} \textit{Before} \\ \textit{If} \\ \textit{Since} \\ \text{etc.} \end{cases}$
[dependent word group] , [full sentence].

2. Dependent word group in the middle:

[First part of complete sentence],
$\begin{cases} \textit{who} \\ \textit{which} \\ \textit{whom} \\ \textit{whose} \end{cases}$
[dependent word group],
[rest of complete sentence].

OR

[First part of complete sentence]
$\begin{cases} \textit{who} \\ \textit{which} \\ \textit{that} \\ \textit{whose} \end{cases}$
[dependent word group]
[rest of complete sentence].

Remember: sometimes you need commas around the dependent section appearing within a complete sentence. At other times you do not. See **12b(1).**

3. Dependent word group at the end:

[Full sentence]
$\begin{cases} \textit{because} \\ \textit{when} \\ \textit{which} \\ \text{etc.} \end{cases}$
[dependent word group].

6d RUN-ON SENTENCES

Run-on sentences are sentences that are not combined correctly. The suggestions in **6c** should help you avoid run-on problems. But here are some specifics about common run-on errors and how to correct them.

6d(1) Fused Sentences

Fused sentences are two sentences put together without any linking words or any punctuation.

> Juan Montez speaks both Spanish and English his family moved to the United States from Mexico eight years ago.

To correct: Either separate the two sentences or add the needed linking words and punctuation.

> Juan Montez speaks both Spanish and English. *His* family moved to the United States from Mexico eight years ago.

> Juan Montez speaks both Spanish and English *because* his family moved to the United States from Mexico eight years ago.

6d(2) Comma Splices

Comma splices are two or more complete sentences put together with just a comma.

> Maria Lonedeer attends tribal meetings, she is proud of her heritage.

To correct: Separate the sentences with a period, replace the comma with a semicolon, or use a joining word.

> Maria Lonedeer attends tribal meetings. She is proud of her heritage.

> Maria Lonedeer attends tribal meetings; she is proud of her heritage.

> Maria Lonedeer attends tribal meetings *because* she is proud of her heritage.

6e TANGLED SENTENCES

Sentences become tangled when the sentence switches direction in the middle. The switch in direction may happen in a number of different ways. One common way occurs when a single word or group of words is used as part of two separate thoughts.

> Daniel Defoe wrote the novel *Robinson Crusoe* tells the story of a man shipwrecked on a deserted island.

To correct: The phrase "the novel *Robinson Crusoe*" serves as both the object of the first part of the tangled sentence and the subject of the second part. Rewrite the tangled sentence as two separate sentences or make one part of the sentence dependent on the other.

> Daniel Defoe wrote the novel *Robinson Crusoe*. **The novel** tells the story of a man shipwrecked on a deserted island.

> Daniel Defoe wrote the novel *Robinson Crusoe,* **which** tells the story of a man shipwrecked on a deserted island.

Sentences also become tangled when two similar phrases are confused.

> Through his adventures, Robinson Crusoe learns that he is capable to take care of himself.

To correct: The sentence confuses the two phrases *capable of taking care* and *able to take care*. Rewrite the sentence to use only one phrase or the other.

> Through his adventures, Robinson Crusoe learns that he is *capable of taking care* of himself.

> Through his adventures, Robinson Crusoe learns that he is *able to take care* of himself.

Finally, sentences can become tangled when a dependent word group is put at the beginning of the sentence and the writer forgets to include a subject for the independent word group.

> Because Crusoe kept a detailed diary, could look back on his accomplishments.

To correct: Add a subject to the independent word group.

> Because Crusoe kept a detailed diary, *he* could look back on his accomplishments.

6f MISPLACED AND DANGLING DESCRIPTIVE WORDS

Watch where you place descriptive words and word groups. They should appear next to the words they describe. Each of the following sentences means something different simply because of the position of the word *only*.

Only the karate champion could smash bricks with her hand. (No other person could do this.)

The *only* karate champion could smash bricks with her hand. (There was no other karate champion.)

The karate champion could *only* smash bricks with her hand. (She had no other skills.)

The karate champion could smash *only* bricks with her hand. (She could not smash other things.)

The karate champion could smash bricks *only* with her hand. (She could not use any other part of her body to do this.)

The karate champion could smash bricks with *only* her hand. (She did not need the help of anything else.)

The karate champion could smash bricks with her *only* hand. (She had just one hand.)

Sentences often change their meaning when a descriptive word group is in the wrong place.

In the large carton, Sarah found her missing clothes.

This says that Sarah is in the carton. The describing words *in the large carton* are in the wrong place.

Sarah found **her missing clothes** *in the large carton.*

This sentence is correct: *in the large carton* tells where the clothes were.

Often *ing* and *ed* word groups "dangle" because writers place them next to the wrong word. Dangling words (dangling modifiers) either describe the wrong thing or they describe nothing at all.

Weighing ninety-seven pounds, football was too dangerous for James.

This says that football, the game, weighs ninety-seven pounds.

Weighing ninety-seven pounds, **James** found football too dangerous.

This sentence is correct: it says *James* weighs ninety-seven pounds.

Frightened by the police, the sewer hid the robbers.

This says that the sewer was frightened by the police.

Frightened by the police, **the robbers** hid in the sewer.

Here we see that the *robbers* were frightened. This sentence is correct.

To correct misplaced descriptive words:

▶ Place descriptive words as close as possible to the word they describe.

▶ If the misplaced descriptive word group begins with the *ing* or *ed* form of a verb:

1. Put the word being described right after the descriptive word group.

   Weighing ninety-seven pounds, **James** found football too dangerous.

2. Rewrite the descriptive word group to include the word being described.

   Because **James** *weighed only ninety-seven pounds,* he found football too dangerous.

6g SOME POINTERS ON SENTENCE FORM

▶ *Do not leave out needed words.*

WRONG | Officer reported suspect left Empire State Building nine o'clock.
RIGHT | *The* officer reported *that the* suspect left *the* Empire State Building *at* nine o'clock.

▶ *Complete all comparisons.*

WRONG | This year the women's tennis tournament was more exciting.
RIGHT | This year the women's tennis tournament was more exciting *than the men's tournament.*

▶ *If you list words or phrases in a series, make each item in the list similar to the others in grammar and logic* (parallelism). By keeping the items in the list parallel, you help the reader see how the items fit together.

WRONG | For dinner we had French onion soup, thick steaks, fresh corn on the cob, giant salads, strawberry shortcake, and soft background music.
RIGHT | For dinner we had French onion soup, thick steaks, fresh corn on the cob, giant salads, *and* strawberry shortcake; soft background music *filled the air.*

The items you use in a series can be the names of things, as in the example just above, which lists a series of objects for the verb *had*. The basic structure of that sentence is:

We [subject] had [verb] { soup [object]
steaks [object]
corn [object]
salads [object]
shortcake. [object]

You can also list any other sentence parts such as subjects, verbs, adjectives, or prepositional phrases. You can even add whole sentences together in series. However, in each case, you must make sure the items in the list are parallel. Each item in the list must be of the same kind. For example, look at the following sentences. Although the sentence structures vary, the items in each list are parallel.

Presidents Fillmore, Garfield, and *Harding* have little fame.

subject
subject } verb   object
subject

The cheetah *spotted, chased,* and *attacked* its prey.

            verb
subject { verb } object
            verb

Because *the temperature is high, humidity is low,* and *winds are heavy,* we may have a dust storm.

dependent { subject   verb   verb completer
linking   { subject   verb   verb completer } subject verb object
word   { subject   verb   verb completer

Now compare this example of a list in which the items are *not* parallel:

WRONG   The invader from outer space burned down Los
             Angeles, blew up Houston, destroyed New York,
             and to *annihilate* Chicago.

To correct: All the items in the list have verbs that go with the subject *the invader,* except for the last item, which has an infinitive. Change the last item to use a parallel verb form, *annihilated.*

RIGHT   The invader from outer space *burned* down Los
             Angeles, *blew up* Houston, *destroyed* New York,
             and *annihilated* Chicago.

Here is another example of an item that does not match the
others in the list:

WRONG   During an inflation, prices increase, wages go up,
             but value of money going down.

To correct: The first two items in the list are independent word
groups, but the last is not. Change to make them all independent.

RIGHT   During an inflation, *prices increase, wages go up,*
             but *the value of money goes down.*

▶ *Vary sentence lengths and types.* If all your sentences follow
the same pattern, your readers may find them boring and hard
to follow. Try to mix long and short, simple and combined
sentences together.

POOR   The first computers used mechanical parts. The
             next computers used vacuum tubes. The next com-
             puters used transistors. The next computers used
             silicone chips. Computers now use thousands of
             integrated circuits on a single chip.
BETTER   Although the first computers used only mechani-
             cal parts, later models switched to electricity with
             vacuum tubes and then transistors. The transistors
             were then miniaturized and combined into inte-
             grated circuits on silicone chips. A single silicone
             chip now can hold thousands of circuits.

7

Verbs

7a WHAT IS A VERB?

The **verb** is the word (or words) that tells what the subject of the sentence does. The verb tells the action of the sentence. Sometimes the action is full of motion, as in this sentence:

> The player *cuts, fakes,* and *shoots* a basket.

Sometimes the action only shows how a thing is or exists, as in these examples.

> The patient *appears* healthy.

> The test results *were* negative.

If you are not sure whether a word is the verb of a sentence, put *I, you,* and *it* in front of the word, one at a time. If any of the resulting word groups makes sense as a sentence, the word is a verb.

> **tree:** I *tree?* You *tree?* (Not a verb)

> **wrestle:** I *wrestle.* You *wrestle.* (Verb)

> **see:** I *see.* You *see.* (Verb)

7b AGREEMENT OF SUBJECT AND VERB

The form of the verb changes in the present tense, depending on who does the action and when the action takes place. When one person or thing does an action, the verb that shows the action must be singular. Most singular verbs in the present tense end in *s.*

> The boy *sings.*

> He *laughs.*

When more than one person or thing does an action, the verb that shows the action must be plural. Plural verbs in the present tense do not end in *s*.

> Boys *sing.*
>
> They *laugh.*

There are some exceptions to this rule. In the present tense, the words *I* and *you* always work with a verb without an *s* ending.

> I *sing.*   You *sing.*
>
> I *laugh.*   You *laugh.*

When you use the helping verb *do* in front of another verb, only this helping verb changes form with different subjects (*do, does*). The second, main verb does not add an *s* for the singular.

> He *agrees.*   He *does agree.*   They *do agree.*

The helping verb *do* is used for emphasis, for negatives, and for questions.

> I *do agree.*   He *does agree.*
>
> I *do* not *agree.*   He *does* not *agree.*
>
> *Do* I *agree?*   *Does* he *agree?*

Some verbs have the same form for singular and plural in the present tense. These verbs include *can, may, must, ought,* and *will.*

> I *must.*   We *must.*
>
> He *must.*   They *must.*

These verbs (modal verbs) are often used as helping verbs. In such verb combinations, as with *do* above, the verbs appearing after the first helping verb do not change form for singular or plural.

> He *must go.*   They *must go.*
>
> He *can be going.*   They *can be going.*

Here are a few more examples of subject-verb agreement in the present tense:

> I *go.*   I *do go.*   I *can go.*
>
> You *go.*   You *do go.*   You *can go.*
>
> She, he, it *goes.*   She, he, it *does go.*   She, he, it *can go.*

We *go*.	We *do go*.	We *can go*.
They *go*.	They *do go*.	They *can go*.

Remember: in tenses other than the present, the verb usually does not change form with different subjects. The verb *to be* is an exception to these rules of agreement, however. It has its own set of singular and plural forms, which are given in the chart below.

FORMS OF THE VERB *TO BE*

The verb *to be* has many different forms and causes agreement problems in the past tense as well as the present. You must learn these forms:

Present

I *am*	I *am* hungry.
you *are*	You *are* friendly.
he *is*, she *is*, it *is*	She *is* happy.
we *are*	We *are* finished.
they *are*	They *are* late.

Past

I *was*	I *was* here.
you *were*	You *were* right.
he *was,* she *was,* it *was*	He *was* tense.
we *were*	We *were* in agreement.
they *were*	They *were* crazy.

In the perfect tenses use the form *been* with the correct helping verbs *has, have,* or *had.*

John *has been* angry for an hour.

They *have been* away for a week.

Regina *had been* arrested before then.

Warning: *be* cannot by itself be used as a verb, except as a command. A sentence like *He be here* is not correct. A command, such as *Be ready by three o'clock,* is however correct.

The toy *can be* fixed.

I plan *to be* at the park.

Singular or Plural?

In some cases it isn't easy to tell whether a verb should be singular or plural. The following rules can help you to make up your mind.

▶ If two or more subjects are added together, use the plural verb.

Basketball and hockey **attract** large crowds.

▶ If you have a choice of subjects in an *either . . . or* (or *neither . . . nor*) word group, use a verb that works with the subject nearer the verb.

Either *five pieces* of gum or one coconut *bar* **costs** a quarter.

▶ To decide whether to use *there is* or *there are* (or *here is* or *here are*), check the subject that comes after the verb.

There *is* one *can* of beans on the shelf.

There *are* twelve *cans* of soup.

▶ In a dependent word group beginning with *who, which,* or *that,* check the word that *who, which,* or *that* refers to and make the verb agree with it.

The sewing *machine, which* still **works,** now sits in the closet.

The *marbles, which are* Alice's prize possession, fall out of the drawer and roll into the corners of the room.

▶ Don't be confused by word groups that come between the subject and the verb. The verb must agree with the subject, not with the extra words that come between the subject and the verb.

The *child* on roller skates *falls* on the pavement.

The *books* given to the library *sit* in the storage room.

▶ *Anyone, anybody, anything, everyone, everybody, everything, nobody, nothing, someone, somebody,* and *something* used as subjects take singular verbs.

Something *happens.*

Everyone *knows.*

Nobody *cares.*

▶ Group words (like *class, team, family,* and *army*) usually take singular verbs because each group is one unit.

The *class votes* to take the day off.

The *team leaves* tomorrow.

7C   VERB TENSES

The ability of the verb to show time is called **tense.** We generally show tense by changing the form of the basic verb word.

The basic verb word is called an **infinitive** when it has a *to* in front of it; for example, *to walk* and *to climb* are the infinitives of the basic verb words *walk* and *climb.* The infinitive never changes form. The infinitive cannot by itself be the main verb in a sentence. Each of the following sentences uses the infinitive *to go,* but it is not the main verb.

They *want* to go.

They *wanted* to go.

The form of the verb can tell the reader whether the action takes place in the past, the present, or the future. Other verb tenses can show more precise time ideas, as the table on pages 79–80 shows. Look at the table before you go on.

To make the past tense, you usually add *d* or *ed* to the verb. To make the perfect tenses, you usually use *have, has,* or *had* with the form of the verb that ends in *d* or *ed.*

Remember: when you have verb phrases made up of several verbs, only the first verb changes form with tense.

She *has* been writing.

She *had* been writing.

Many verbs work in special ways. They do not follow the usual rules when they change tense. For the irregular verbs in the list at right,

▶ use the verb form from column A to make the present and future tenses.

▶ use the verb form from column B to make the past tense.

▶ use the verb form from column C to make the perfect tenses— and be sure to use *have, has,* or *had* with it.

Common Irregular Verb Forms

A Present	B Past	C Perfect
awake	awoke	awaked
beat	beat	beaten
become	became	become
begin	began	begun
bend	bent	bent
bet	bet	bet
bite	bit	bitten
bleed	bled	bled
blow	blew	blown
bring	brought	brought
burst	burst	burst
buy	bought	bought
catch	caught	caught
choose	chose	chosen
come	came	come
cost	cost	cost
cut	cut	cut
dig	dug	dug
do	did	done
draw	drew	drawn
drink	drank	drunk
drive	drove	driven
eat	ate	eaten
fall	fell	fallen
feed	fed	fed
feel	felt	felt
fight	fought	fought
find	found	found
fly	flew	flown
forget	forgot	forgotten
freeze	froze	frozen
get	got	gotten, got
give	gave	given
go	went	gone
grow	grew	grown
hang	hung	hung
have	had	had
hide	hid	hidden
hit	hit	hit
hold	held	held

(The Common Irregular Verb Forms list continues on page 82.)

FORMATION OF VERB TENSES

	Use	*How to Form*
Present	to show what happens now or can happen at any time	the present form of the verb (add *s* or *es* for all singular subjects except *I* and *you:* see **7b**)
Past	to show what happened at a fixed time in the past	the verb + *d* or *ed* (see list on pages 79, 82–83 for irregular forms)
Future	to show what will happen in the future	*will* + present form of the verb
Present Perfect	to show what has happened in the past and continues in the present; to show what happened in the past, but at no particular time	*have* (or *has* for all singular subjects except *I* and *you*) + *d* or *ed* form of the verb (see list on pages 79, 81–83 for irregular forms)
Past Perfect	to show an action in the past that happened even before another event in the past	*had* + *d* or *ed* form of verb (see list on pages 79, 81–83 for irregular forms)
Future Perfect	to show something that has not yet been done but that will be done before a set time in the future	*will have* + *d* or *ed* form of verb (see list on pages 79, 81–83 for irregular forms)
Present Continuous	to show an event that is going on right now	*am, is* (for singular subjects) or *are* (for plural subjects and *you*) + verb with *ing* ending
Past Continuous	to show an event that was going on when something else happened	*was* (for singular subjects) or *were* (for plural subjects and *you*) + verb with *ing* ending
Future Continuous	to show an event that will be going on when something else happens	*will be* + *ing* form of verb

FORMATION OF VERB TENSES (*cont.*)

Example	Sentence Example
sleep	*Now I* **sleep.**
works	*The washer* **works.**
	We **work** *as mail carriers.*
talked	*Yesterday Lenora* **talked** *with Harold.*
will fly	*In the future, rockets* **will fly** *to Mars every week.*
have lived	*I* **have lived** *in this house for seven years.*
has moaned	*The cat* **has moaned** *for ten minutes in the rain.*
had stopped	*The car* **had stopped** *before the truck hit it.*
will have completed	*By tomorrow Steve* **will have completed** *the term paper.*
am building	*I* **am building** *a table.*
is building	*Luisa* **is building** *a robot in the garage.*
are building	*She and her sister* **are building** *a model plane.*
was rowing	*I* **was rowing** *on Massapequa Lake when it began to rain.*
were rowing	*Sarah and Maxine* **were rowing** *swiftly when their oars broke.*
will be reading	*The guard* **will be reading** *a newspaper when we sneak up on him.*

Common Irregular Verb Forms (*cont from page 79.*)

A Present	B Past	C Perfect
hurt	hurt	hurt
keep	kept	kept
know	knew	known
lay	laid	laid
lead	led	led
leave	left	left
lend	lent	lent
let	let	let
lie	lay	lain
light	lighted, lit	lighted, lit
lose	lost	lost
make	made	made
mean	meant	meant
meet	met	met
put	put	put
quit	quit	quit
read	read	read
ride	rode	ridden
ring	rang	rung
rise	rose	risen
run	ran	run
see	saw	seen
sell	sold	sold
send	sent	sent
shake	shook	shaken
shine	shone	shone
shoot	shot	shot
show	showed	shown
shrink	shrank	shrunk
shut	shut	shut
sing	sang	sung
sink	sank	sunk
sit	sat	sat
sleep	slept	slept
slide	slid	slid
speak	spoke	spoken
speed	sped	sped
spend	spent	spent
spin	spun	spun
spring	sprang	sprung
stand	stood	stood
steal	stole	stolen

Common Irregular Verb Forms (*cont.*)

A Present	B Past	C Perfect
stick	stuck	stuck
sting	stung	stung
strike	struck	struck
swear	swore	sworn
sweep	swept	swept
swim	swam	swum
swing	swung	swung
take	took	taken
teach	taught	taught
tear	tore	torn
tell	told	told
think	thought	thought
throw	threw	thrown
wear	wore	worn
weave	wove	woven
weep	wept	wept
win	won	won
wind	wound	wound
wring	wrung	wrung
write	wrote	written

7d   ACTIVE AND PASSIVE VERBS

For **active** verbs the doer of the action is the subject of the sentence.

*Harriet **installs** the new program on her computer.*

Passive, on the other hand, means "quietly receiving." With passive verbs the receiver of the action is the subject of the sentence.

*The new program **was installed** by Harriet on her computer.*

The passive form of a verb includes part of the verb *to be (am, is, are, was, were, will be)* and the form of the verb used in perfect tenses. (For irregular verbs see column C in the list on pages 79, 81–83.)

Generally, passive verbs are less direct and are wordier than active verbs. In most cases you should write active, rather than passive, sentences.

PASSIVE	*receiver* The extra furniture *is stored* in the attic by the *doer* Brown family.
ACTIVE	*doer* *receiver* The Brown family *stores* extra furniture in the attic.
PASSIVE	*receiver* The car *was driven* over thirty thousand miles last *doer* year by the traveling salesperson.
ACTIVE	*doer* *receiver* The traveling salesperson *drove* the car over thirty thousand miles last year.

7e   NEEDLESS SHIFTS IN TENSE

Sometimes you need to shift one tense to another in a sentence or in a paragraph. But you can confuse readers if you shift tense without any real reason. Look at this example:

> (1) Tony *stormed* into the room and he *looks* at nobody. (2) His mouth *twitches* in anger. (3) Finally he *spoke*. (4) He *asks*, "Who *wants* to tell me what *happened* to my car?"

These sentences shift tense without any reason. In sentence 1 *stormed* is a past tense verb—but *looks* is in the present tense. Why? In sentence 2 *twitches* is a present tense verb, but in sentence 3 *spoke* is in the past. In sentence 4 the writer uses *asks,* present tense again. Look at the sentences correctly written:

> (1) Tony *stormed* into the room and he *looked* at nobody. (2) His mouth *twitched* in anger. (3) Finally he *spoke*. (4) He *asked,* "Who *wants* to tell me what *happened* to my car?"

Notice that the present tense verbs were changed to the past tense. In the statement Tony makes in sentence 4, however, the tense shift is all right. First, Tony's words are quoted exactly. Next, he asks a question in the present tense ("Who *wants*") about an event that occurred in the past ("what *happened*"). There is a reason to shift tenses.

┌─── **WATCH YOUR VERB ENDINGS: A REVIEW CHART** ───┐

▶ Use an *s* or *es* at the end of almost all verbs in the present tense that go with *he, she, it,* one person's name, or the name of one thing.

He *goes* away.   (NOT He go away.)

John *runs* from his aunt.   (NOT John run from his aunt.)

The book *sits* on the chair.   (NOT The book sit on the chair.)

▶ Do not use *s* at the end of verbs that go with *I, you, we, they,* more than one person's name, or the names of more than one thing.

I *go* away.   (NOT I goes away.)

We *run* from Aunt Jane.   (NOT We runs from Aunt Jane.)

Roberta and Mark *sit* on the bench.   (NOT Roberta and Mark sits on the bench.)

▶ Put a *d* or *ed* at the end of a verb to form the past tense of all regular verbs used with any subject.

I *dressed* quickly.

He *dressed* quickly.

We *dressed* quickly.

▶ Put a *d* or *ed* at the end of a verb to form the perfect tenses of all regular verbs used with any subject.

Roberta and Mark have *dressed.*

Jane has *dressed.*

We all had *dressed* by then.

▶ Put a *d* or an *ed* at the end of a verb to make the passive form of all regular verbs used with a form of the verb *to be.*

The baby *was dressed* by her father.

▶ Put a *d*, an *ed*, or an *ing* at the end of all regular verbs used as adjectives (see page 95.)

the *unlisted* number   the *calling* person

the *interrupted* call   the *interrupting* call

▶ Use the forms of irregular verbs according to the explanation on pages 79, 81–83.

▶ Use the forms of the verb *to be* according to the explanation on page 76.

8

Pronouns

Pronouns are words that take the place of names of persons or objects.

> Psychology is the study of human minds. *It* is a social science.
>
> Mary likes chocolate mints. *She* eats *them* every night.

In the first sentence *it* is a pronoun; it takes the place of *psychology*. In the second sentence *she* takes the place of *Mary,* and *them* takes the place of *chocolate mints.* Both *she* and *them* are pronouns.

8a   PRONOUN REFERENCES

Use the name of a person or an object at least once before you use a pronoun because it must always be clear which word the pronoun replaces. In the following example, the pronouns *her* and *she* refer to *Jane Austen. Them* refers to her novels.

> Jane Austen wrote *her* novels in the early nineteenth century. In *them, she* described middle- and upper-class British life at that time.

If there is any chance the reader will get confused, either because the pronoun is too far away from the word it replaces or because the pronoun might refer to a word it is not meant to replace, you should not use a pronoun. In the following example, the reader does not know who enjoyed the experience: the boys, the girls, or both.

| UNCLEAR | The boys chatted with the girls; they liked it. |
| BETTER | The boys chatted with the girls; they all liked it. |

Make sure you use the right pronoun for the persons or things you are describing. If you shift pronouns, it may seem as if you are writing about something new.

| WEAK | *College students* have difficult lives. *I* have to work hard. *You* have to be motivated. |
| IMPROVED | *College students* have difficult lives. *They* have to work hard. *They* have to be motivated. |

8b   PRONOUNS AND GENDER

Be sure not to use the male pronouns *he, him,* and *his* when the individual described may be either male or female. You may use the phrases *he or she, him or her, his or her.* You may make the whole sentence plural and use *they, them, their.* Or you may rewrite the sentence to avoid the pronoun. Do not, however, use a plural pronoun if the rest of the sentence remains singular.

WRONG	If *a student* wishes to apply for a loan, *he* should complete an application.
WRONG	If *a student* wishes to apply for a loan, *they* should complete an application.
RIGHT	If *a student* wishes to apply for a loan, *he or she* should complete an application.
RIGHT	If *students wish* to apply for *loans, they* should complete *applications.*
RIGHT	*A student who wishes to apply for a loan* should complete an application.

8c   PRONOUNS AS SUBJECTS AND OBJECTS

A pronoun can be *singular* or *plural:* it can take the place of one thing or it can take the place of many things. Certain pronouns, however, are always singular: *anyone, everyone, someone, no one, none, anybody, everybody, nobody,* and *somebody.*

Most pronouns change form depending on their place in the sentence, as described on page 88.

As a subject	As an object
I	me
we	us
you	you
he	him
she	her
it	it
they	them
who	whom

Use the **subject form** of the pronoun when:

▶ the pronoun is the subject of the sentence.

She eats lunch.

They screamed.

The pronoun may be part of a double subject, so be careful.

Annette and *she* eat lunch.

▶ the pronoun comes after a form of the verb *to be* (see **7c**).

The winner was *she.*

It was *I* who spoke.

▶ the pronoun is part of a comparison sentence and is parallel to the subject of the sentence.

Francine programs computers better than *I.*

Use the **object form** of the pronoun when:

▶ the pronoun is an object of the sentence (see **6a**).

Antoine pushed *him.*

▶ the pronoun comes after a word that shows direction or relationship like *behind, to, from, in, on, above, below, near, with,* and *beside.* (See Chapter 10 for more on prepositions.)

Bring the book to *me.*

He sang with *her.*

The dog sat beside *him.*

Remember: even if the pronoun is part of a double object, you still use the object form.

Fran stood between Fred and *me.*

Students often have problems in deciding which pronoun to use when a double subject or double object appears in a sentence. To avoid such problems, take one word in the double subject or object at a time.

Stella and _____ drove to school yesterday.

If you do not know, for example, whether to use *him* or *he* in the blank, first think, "*Stella* drove to school." Then think, "*Him* drove to school." That doesn't sound right. Only *"He* drove to school" sounds right. Now return to the sentence with the blank and fill in the correct word:

> Stella and *he* drove to school yesterday.

If you do not know whether to use *him* or *he* in the following blank, take one word at a time:

> They drove to school with Stella and _____.

First think, "They drove to school with *Stella.*" Then think, "They drove to school with *he.*" That doesn't sound right. Only, "They drove to school with *him*" sounds right. Now return to the sentence with the blank and fill in the correct word:

> They drove to school with Stella and *him.*

8d PRONOUNS THAT SHOW OWNERSHIP

The following possessive forms of the pronouns show that the person or thing replaced by the pronoun owns something:

> my, mine
> our, ours
> your, yours
> his
> her, hers
> its
> their, theirs

> | | | |
> |---|---|---|
> | *his* cat | *her* dog | The hat is *yours.* |
> | *my* goldfish | *their* monkey | The coat is *mine.* |

Remember: do not use an apostrophe with a pronoun that shows ownership. If you write *it's,* you mean "it is." However, an apostrophe is required to show ownership with words such as *anyone's, everyone's, somebody's, nobody's.*

8e PRONOUNS THAT RELATE

Some pronouns—called relative pronouns—connect the names of persons or things with expanded descriptions or other statements about those persons or things. They indicate how groups of words relate to one or more other words within a sentence. Relative pronouns serve as dependent linking words (see **6c(3)**). *Who, which,* and *that* are relative pronouns.

> The actors *who* were nominated for the award were all first-time nominees.

> The crowd gave standing ovations to all the actors *who* were nominated for the award.

The dependent clause *who were nominated for the award* tells more about the actors, referred to by the relative pronoun *who.*

> The very last question, *which* certainly stumped me, was added at the last minute.

> Other students had problems with the very last question, which certainly stumped me.

The dependent clause *which certainly stumped me* tells more about the question, referred to by the relative pronoun *which.*

> The dog *that* saved the child had been with the family for many years.

> The mayor awarded the dog *that* saved the child a medal and a year's supply of dog biscuits.

The dependent clause *that saved the child* tells more about the dog, referred to by the pronoun *that.*

Use *who* to refer to people and *which* or *that* to refer to places, things, or ideas. Notice, however, that in each example above, the relative pronoun was the subject in the dependent clause:

> *who* [the actors] were nominated

> *which* [the question] certainly stumped me

> *that* [the dog] saved the child

A relative pronoun can also be an object in a dependent clause:

> The actors *whom* the judges nominated were all well-known stars.

Whom is the object of the verb *nominated* in the dependent clause (*the judges nominated whom*).

> The question for *which* there was no answer puzzled everyone.

Which is the object of *for* in the prepositional phrase *for which,* part of the dependent clause *for which there was no answer.*

I have a receipt for the beagle *that* the breeder sold me.

That is the object of the verb *sold* in the dependent clause (*the breeder sold me that*).

Note, also, that the subject and object forms are the same for *which* and *that*. Only for humans is there a change of form: we use *who* for a subject and *whom* for an object.

Finally, use the possessive form *whose* for all persons, places, objects, or ideas to show ownership.

> Actors *whose* films are available on video continue to be known to audiences.

> The question *whose* answer could not be determined was not counted in the final grade.

> The terrier *whose* collar had the owner's phone number was returned.

For the rule on when to use commas with relative clauses, see **12b(1).**

GUIDE TO USING PRONOUNS

▶ Make sure it is clear to which word the pronoun refers.

▶ Use the form of the pronoun (singular or plural; male, female, or neuter) that agrees with the noun referred to.

▶ Avoid using only a male pronoun when referring to a person who could be male or female. Use *he or she,* change the whole sentence to plural, or select a genderless alternative like *person.*

▶ Use the subject, object, or ownership form depending on the pronoun's role in the sentence.

9

Adjectives and Adverbs

Adjectives are words that give more information about nouns (that is, about names of persons, places, or things); **adverbs** are words that tell more about verbs and adjectives. Look at this example:

> An honest politician never lies.

The words *an* and *honest* are adjectives. They let you know how many politicians (*an*) and what kind of politician (*honest*). Adjectives usually tell *what kind, what size, what color, how many,* or *which one.* The word *never* is an adverb. It lets you know when the action of the verb (*lies*) takes place (*never*). Adverbs usually tell *when, how, where,* or *to what extent.*

Do not confuse adjectives and adverbs. Use only adjectives to describe nouns and only adverbs to describe verbs and adjectives. Adjectives almost never end in *ly,* but most adverbs do end in *ly.* In fact, many adjectives can be changed into adverbs simply by adding *ly* (for example, *kind, kindly; slow, slowly; easy, easily*). Study the following examples:

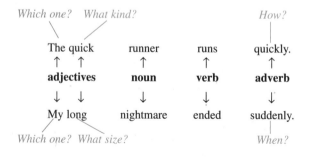

Be especially careful in using the adjectives *good* and *bad* and the adverbs *well* and *badly* (see pages 108, 111).

The main purpose of some sentences is to tell you more about the noun that is the subject of the sentence. Such sentences usually have verbs such as *is, looks, feels, seems, becomes,* or *smells.* Use an adjective after these verbs to complete the information about the noun, as in these examples:

> The cheese looks *green.* (What color?)
>
> The meat smells *rotten.* (What kind?)
>
> The mess becomes *enormous.* (What size?)

In each case, the adjective describes the noun that stands before the verb.

9a   SINGULAR AND PLURAL ADJECTIVES

9a(1)   Adjectives with Singular Nouns

Adjectives such as *a, an, this, that, one, any, every, each, another,* and *much* describe only one thing. The noun that follows must be singular. In addition, when you use a singular noun, you usually must use one of these singular adjectives, the word *the,* or a word showing ownership (such as *my* or *John's*) in front of the singular noun. For example:

> *a* party, *this* party, *each* party, *another* party, *the* party, *Carol's* party

Proper names, such as those of people, places, institutions, or holidays, can be used without a singular adjective or a word showing ownership in front of them. Note these examples:

> Andrea, Kensington Park, Iowa State University, Thanksgiving

Other nouns that do not need a singular adjective or a word showing ownership in front of them identify things or ideas that are not counted or countable. Study these examples:

> wheat, advice, truth, honesty, weather

Notice where *a, an,* and *the* are used or not used in the following examples:

> *The* diamond was smaller than *a* grain of wheat, but in *the* machine it caused damage beyond belief.

Malvina, *a* young woman from *an* island off *the* coast, moved to *the* mainland for further education without leaving North Carolina.

The words *a* and *an* refer to any single example of the category being named by the noun that follows, but not to a particular item from within that category. *An orange* or *a bottle*, for instance, means "any orange" or "any bottle." Use the word *an* before words that begin with the sound of the letters *a, e, i, o,* or *u.* Use the word *a* before all other words. Notice that the beginning sound of the word is important, not the actual letter that starts the word. Study these examples:

*a c*oconut	*an h*our
*an a*vocado	*an e*xcellent coconut
an F	*a g*reen avocado
*a h*alf	*a B*

Use the word *the* in front of singular nouns (even proper nouns and collective nouns) to refer to a whole class or category of things or to any particular single item in that category. Here are some examples:

The orange is one type of citrus fruit.

The orange I ate this morning was fresh.

The George Saunders who came to my office was *the same* George Saunders I knew in elementary school.

The herd was split into two smaller herds.

9a(2)   Adjectives with Plural Nouns

Plural nouns do not have *a* or *an* in front of them. However, other adjectives do provide additional information about plural nouns.

Pictures can help *students* understand *ideas.*

These old pictures can help *the students* in this class understand *many ideas* about history.

The word *the* can also be used with plural nouns to identify specific items.

The pictures on *the handouts* illustrate *the concepts* of affiliation and alienation.

Adjectives such as *these, those, all, several, many, two,* and *three* describe more than one thing. The noun that follows them must be plural. Use an adjective with a plural noun only to give more information.

Pencils always break.

Cheap pencils always break.

These cheap pencils always break.

9b   ADJECTIVES MADE FROM VERBS

The *ing* and *ed* forms of verbs are often used as adjectives. Compare the phrases *the depressing news* and *the depressed man, the exciting game* and *the excited crowd*. Be sure not to confuse the meanings of the *ing* and the *ed* forms. The *ing* form lets you know that the noun is actively doing what the adjective describes. The *ed* form usually means the action is being done to the noun (see **7d**). See how the two forms develop in the following examples.

The news depressed the man.
The news was *depressing*. The *depressing* news came as a surprise.
The man was *depressed*. The *depressed* man cried.

The game excites the crowd.
The game is *exciting*. The *exciting* game ends.
The crowd is *excited*. The *excited* crowd cheers.

Whenever you use verb forms as adjectives, be sure to use the correct endings. See pages 79, 81–83 for the forms of irregular verbs.

9c   COMPARISONS USING ADJECTIVES AND ADVERBS

Adjectives and adverbs can be used to compare two or more things or actions.

The Hancock Tower is *taller* than the World Trade Center.

Jan eats *more* hungrily than John.

When comparing two items, add either an *er* at the end of the adjective or adverb or the word *more* before the adjective or adverb. Do not use both at the same time. Use the *er* ending when the word is short; use the word *more* when the word is long or harder to pronounce.

When comparing three or more items, either add an *est* to the end of the adjective or adverb or put the word *most* before the adjective or adverb, depending on the length of the word. Do not use both the *est* ending and *most*.

Look at the following examples:

happy	happier	happiest
happily	more happily	most happily
excited	more excited	most excited
excitedly	more excitedly	most excitedly
early	earlier	earliest

A few words have unusual forms for comparison:

good	better	best
well	better	best
bad	worse	worst
badly	worse	worst

When you write comparisons, make sure they are complete (see **6g**).

10

Prepositions and Prepositional Phrases

A **preposition** is a word that goes before a noun or pronoun to make a phrase that acts as an adjective or adverb. The preposition shows how the noun or pronoun is related to the rest of the sentence. For example, look at the following sentence:

> Marilyn parked the car in the garage.

The word *in* is a preposition; *in the garage* is a prepositional phrase. The word *in* shows the connection between the garage and the main action of the sentence—parking the car. It tells *where* she parked the car and so acts as an adverb. In the following sentence, the same prepositional phrase *in the garage* serves as an adjective.

> The car *in the garage* has a flat tire.

This phrase is an adjective because it identifies *which* car is discussed.

Prepositions Used Most Often

about	before	for	out
above	behind	from	over
across	below	in	through
after	between	inside	to
against	beyond	into	toward
along	by	near	under
among	despite	of	upon
as	during	on	with
at			

The main difficulty most people have with prepositions is knowing which one to use. In particular, certain prepositions often combine with other kinds of words to make standard phrases. The following list presents some combinations that often cause trouble. There are many other similar combinations in English. If you are uncertain about which preposition to use in a combination, a dictionary may give you help.

Some Preposition Combinations

according *to*
agree *on* a plan
agree *to* a proposal
agree *with* a person
angry *at* an event
angry *with* a person
break *down* a door
capable *of*
charge *for* a purchase
charge *with* a crime
clean *up* a house
conform *to*
die *of*
differ *about* a question (to disagree)
differ *from* (to be not like)
differ *with* a person (to disagree)
different *from*
except *for*
fight *for* a cause
fight *with* a person
identical *with*
independent *of*
inferior *to*
in search *of*
open *up* a store
prefer one thing *to* another
prior *to*
rewarded *by* a person
rewarded *for* a deed
rewarded *with* a prize
shut *down* a machine
similar *to*
superior *to*
wait *at* a place
wait *for* an arrival or event
wait *on* a customer

Prepositions are often used in telling about the **time** when an event takes place. Particular prepositions are used for different units of time.

For weeks, months, seasons, or years, use *in* or *during*.

in January, *during* 1998, *during* the week of July 27, *in* the spring

For specific days of the week, calendar dates, and holidays, use *on*.

> *on* Tuesday, *on* October 15, *on* New Year's Day

For clock times and other specific times of day, use *at*.

> *at* noon, *at* five-thirty, *at* six o'clock, *at* 11:23, *at* sunset

The phrase *on time* refers to scheduled events; *in time* refers to unscheduled events.

> We rushed to be *on time* for the start of the show.
>
> We made it *in time* to say goodbye to Hal.

Prepositions are also used in indicating the duration of an action or event—how long it lasts or continues. The most common prepositions referring to length of time are *for, since, during,* and *from . . . to*.

For and *since* can refer to a period of time.

> I have worked here *for* three years.
>
> I haven't seen him *since* last year.

During indicates an identified time within a larger period of time.

> I will go to the store sometime *during* my work break.

From . . . to marks the beginning and the end of a period of time.

> Salvatore played soccer *from* dawn *to* dusk.

11

Style and Usage

11a SPECIFIC AND GENERAL WORDS

Words that name things do not always tell exactly what the writer means because not all words are **specific** enough. Look at these three words:

> animal   horse   colt

The word *animal* could be used to refer to many different kinds of animals: dogs, humans, cats, monkeys. Any word that does not limit meaning for us is called **general**; general, of course, is the opposite of **specific.**

The word *horse* is more specific than *animal* because it limits the meaning to a particular kind of animal. The word *colt* is better still because it gives an even more specific meaning: a colt is a young male horse. The more specific a word is, usually the more **concrete** it is. Concrete words give specific names for things and are especially helpful in giving readers exact information.

Abstract words are words for ideas, things that cannot be touched or seen. *Patience, fear, love, communism,* and *suffering* are abstract words.

Often we need words for ideas, so it is important to use abstract terms. But even when writers must use an abstract word, they need one that is the most specific in stating an idea. In these sentences, all the emphasized words are abstract:

> He showed *emotion.*
>
> He showed *fear.*
>
> He showed *terror.*

Emotion, fear, and *terror* are all abstract words because they refer to things we cannot touch or hold. But notice how *terror* is the most specific of the abstract words the writer has chosen. *Emotion* is too general: it could mean love, anger, hate, sorrow, or any other strong feeling. *Fear* is better because it limits the kind of emotion the writer wants to tell about. But *terror,* meaning extreme fear, tells exactly what the writer has in mind.

To be specific and concrete:

▶ Think about whether or not the word you have chosen is *exactly* the word you want to use. When you say *nice,* do you mean gentle, thoughtful, or friendly?

▶ Use an exact word whenever you can. Say *hamburger* instead of *meat, spinach* instead of *vegetables, sparrow* instead of *bird.*

▶ Use details of sight, smell, touch, sound, or action.

General	Specific
door	creaking wooden door
building	cool, damp church
bird	fluttering brown wren

▶ Use a dictionary (see **18i**) or a thesaurus to check for specific word meanings, synonyms, and antonyms.

11b REPETITION

Don't use words that repeat each other's meanings.

POOR	the positive advantages and the negative disadvantages
BETTER	the advantages and disadvantages
POOR	I will begin to start to leave.
BETTER	I will start to leave.
BEST	I will leave.
POOR	The reason is because . . .
BETTER	The reason is that . . .
POOR	Where is the book at?
BETTER	Where is the book?

11c WORDINESS

Avoid wordy expressions such as these:

Wordy	More Direct
a great deal of	much, many
at this point in time	now
being as, being that	because, since
bring to your remembrance	remind you
due to the fact that, on account of the fact that, owing to the fact that	because, since
for the purpose of beginning	to begin
He is the kind of person who likes to talk too much.	He talks too much.
in an angry manner, in an angry way	angrily
in between, out behind	between, behind
in order to bring about the desired end of passing	to pass
in reference to, in regard to	about
in the neighborhood of, in the vicinity of	near
of a friendly nature, of a friendly kind	friendly
One of the things that is important to me is my schoolwork.	My schoolwork is important to me.
The question as to whether	whether
The thing which I want to talk about is . . .	I will talk about . . .
The thing is that George will be late.	George will be late.
which is located in	in

11d CLICHÉS AND SLOGANS

Clichés are tired old expressions that no longer carry any strong meaning (for example, *as American as apple pie, wise as an owl,* and *it goes without saying*). Slogans are the catch phrases of different political, social, or other group movements. Look at the following relatively recent American slogans:

leading-edge technology

Information wants to be free.

Let's look at the bottom line.

Moving right along . . .

ghostbusters, crimebusters, dustbusters, heatbusters, etc.

When you write clichés and slogans, neither you nor your reader has to think about your meaning. You are passing up a chance to say something original or more significant.

In the following passage the specific troubles of the writer are lost in a fog of clichés. All we learn is that the writer seems unhappy.

> The stresses and strains of the modern world are just too much for any person to cope with. No wonder I feel stressed out and burned out.

If the writer had thought a little more closely about what she really wanted to communicate, she could have defined her condition more specifically and graphically:

> Being a full-time parent, worker, and student leaves me no time to be good at or enjoy any of those roles. I just run to keep from dropping.

Using about the same number of words, she has told us much more about her situation.

11e SHADES OF MEANING

Use the right word to express your exact meaning. Some words, although they mean nearly the same thing, actually mean separate, distinct things. *Boat,* for example, refers to a small craft that is usually open at the top; *ship,* on the other hand, refers to a large seagoing craft.

The small differences between words help you describe different types of similar things quickly and clearly. There are, for example, many types of boats and ships, and each type is described by a specific word. Here are a few of them:

barge	a roomy, flat-bottomed boat
battleship	a large, heavily armed warship
destroyer	a small, fast warship
dinghy	a small rowboat
freighter	a ship for carrying freight

schooner	a large sailing ship
scow	a square-ended barge for carrying garbage or gravel

Not only technical words have shades of meaning. Even when you are writing about human feelings, you need to pay attention to exact shades of meaning. The following words, for example, all describe some kind of unpleasant feeling, but notice how different each is.

envy	a painful awareness that somebody else has something you want
jealousy	hostility toward a rival
suspicion	distrust
resentment	a feeling that someone has wronged you
grudge	a long-lasting resentment
revenge	desire to hurt someone in return for what he or she has done
malice	desire to do harm for evil pleasure

The best place to find the shades of meaning of any word is in a dictionary (see **18i**).

11f   INCLUSIVE LANGUAGE

Make sure your references to people and groups include all people who appropriately should be included and do not exclude anyone on the basis of race, gender, ethnicity, or other group characteristics. Do not use words that show prejudice against people on the basis of race, sex, national origin, or handicap. Such prejudiced language suggests that all people in a certain group are of lower status than other people. You should avoid insulting words for ethnic or racial groups or for people with handicaps. You should use only words showing respect for individuals in these groups.

Sexist words, however, are sometimes more difficult to spot and avoid than other kinds of prejudiced language. Many words in the English language are based on old notions that only men do certain kinds of jobs and fill certain kinds of roles. Words like *chairman, mailman, weatherman, mankind,* and *forefathers* show a sexist prejudice. Whenever possible, substitute a term that avoids a sexual stereotype, such as *humankind* or *ancestors.* Because terms such as *chairperson, mailperson,* and *weatherperson* may seem awkward, older terms such as *chair* or *head, letter carrier* or *postal clerk,* and *meteorologist* are preferred.

When using pronouns, do not use only male pronouns when the person referred to can be either male or female. Using the phrase *he or she* is acceptable, although sometimes awkward. Rewriting the sentence to make all references plural or to avoid the need for pronouns is usually better. When you are writing a long piece with a number of different pronoun references to different people who may be either male or female, you can also make half the references male and half female. See **8b** for some suggested ways of avoiding sexist pronouns.

11g WORDS COMMONLY CONFUSED

A number of words in English cause problems because they are similar to other words. Here is a list of the most common mistakes.

accept, except

Accept means "to receive willingly."
Except means "leave this one out."

▶ Fran *accepts* the gift.
All my friends *except* Jean wished me a good trip.

adapt, adopt

Adapt means "to change to fit the situation."
Adopt means "to take on as part of oneself."

▶ Kheng *adapted* well to her new job.
She *adopted* a new style of thinking.

advice, advise

Advice is a noun that means "an opinion about what to do."
Advise is a verb that means "to recommend."

▶ Kevin's *advice* was good.
Please *advise* me what to do.

affect, effect

Affect is a verb that means "to change."
Effect is a noun that means "result."

▶ Poor sleep *affects* my mood.
The *effect* of generosity is only sometimes gratitude.

Affect is also a noun that means "feeling."
Effect is also a verb that means "to accomplish."

▶ Winning a competition often is accompanied by the *affect* of elation.
Despite much effort, she could not *effect* the organizational changes that she wanted.

allusion, illusion

An *allusion* is an indirect reference to an idea, person, event, or piece of writing.
An *illusion* is a mistaken perception of reality.

▶ The poem has an *allusion* to Plato's idea of the soul.
The idea that the stock market will never go down is an *illusion*.

almost, most

Almost means "nearly."
Most means "more than half."

▶ The robber took *most* of my money; I was left *almost* penniless.

a lot, alot, allot

Alot is an incorrect spelling for *a lot*. *A lot* or *a lot of* is an informal way of saying *many* or *much*. When writing, you should use *many* or *much*.
Allot is a totally different word meaning "to give out shares."

▶ At the fair *many* prizes were given out.
The judges *allot* one prize to each child.

already, all ready

Already (one word) means "before a specific time."
All ready (two words) means "entirely prepared."

▶ It is only noon, but I am *already* tired.
The dinner is *all ready* and on the table.

alright, all right

Alright is incorrect; use only *all right*.

▶ The movie was *all right*, but it wasn't great.

altogether, **all together**	*Altogether* (one word) means "entirely." *All together* (two words) means "all in one place."

▶ It is *altogether* too hot.
The math teachers sat *all together* at the meeting.

among, between	*Among* implies three or more people or things. *Between* implies only two.

▶ She divided the ice cream *among* the three children.
The alley runs *between* the two houses.

amount, number	Use *amount* for things in bulk. Use *number* for things that can be counted. Similarly, use *little, less,* and *much* for bulk; *few, fewer,* and *many* for counting.

▶ A large *amount* of sugar is in the barrel.
A large *number* of people go hungry every day.

anyone, any one	*Anyone* (one word) means "any person at all." *Any one* (two words) means "any person or thing from a specific group." *Everyone* and *every one, someone* and *some one* follow the same pattern.

▶ Does *anyone* want to wash the dishes?
Does *any one* of you children want to wash the dishes?

as, like	Use *as* for word groups with verbs. Use *like* for word groups without verbs.

▶ Frank practices his flute four hours each day, *as* he must to be successful.
Sherry's small apartment is *like* a large closet.

assure, ensure, insure	*Assure* means "to give confidence to and remove doubt from" a person. *Ensure* means "to make something certain." *Insure* means "to guarantee against loss."

▶ The group leader *assured* the scouts that the trip would not be dangerous.
Careful planning *ensured* the success of the trip.
The scouts *insured* the camp by purchasing a policy.

bad, badly

Bad describes nouns; it is also used after verbs of being, such as *feel* and *look*.
Badly describes verbs.

▶ I had a *bad* time.
The patient looks very *bad*.
Karen plays tennis *badly*.

because of, due to

Due to is too informal for most writing; use *because of*.

▶ *Because of* the high humidity, we fought a constant battle against mold and mildew.

beside, besides

Beside means "next to."
Besides means "in addition to."

▶ The motorcycle is parked *beside* the car.
Besides a car, Deborah owned a motorcycle.

breath, breathe

Breath is a noun that means "a gulp of air."
Breathe is a verb that means "to take in and blow out air."

▶ The doctor told me to *breathe* deeply, so I took a deep *breath*.

can, may

Can means "to be able."
May means "to be permitted."

▶ *Can* I run a mile in under four minutes?
You *may* leave the room if you wish.

casual, causal

Casual means "informal or unplanned."
Causal means "relating to a cause."

▶ The meeting was relaxed and *casual*.
The detective found a *causal* connection between Sym's actions and Linnerby's death.

cite, sight, site

Cite is a verb that means "to refer to a text."
Sight is a noun that means "the ability to see."
Site is a noun that means "a place where something happens or is located."

▶ The lawyer *cited* a Supreme Court opinion.
His *sight* was failing because of glaucoma.
We will build a recreation center at this *site*.

complement, **compliment**	*Complement* means "to fit well with something else."
	Compliment means "to praise someone in person."

▶ Martina *complimented* the designer on how well the color of the dress *complemented* its cut.

conscience, conscious *Conscience* is the ability to recognize right and wrong.

Conscious means "aware or awake."

▶ Her *conscience* told her to give back the money. The boxer was knocked down, but he was still *conscious.*

could have, could've, See *of, have.*
could of

data, media, *Data, media,* and *phenomena* are all plural
phenomena and must use plural verbs. The singular forms are *datum, medium,* and *phenomenon.*

▶ The *data agree* with the theory.
All the various news *media report* that Congress will act.
Electrical *phenomena were* first observed in the eighteenth century.

desert, dessert A *desert* is a dry region.
A *dessert* is a sweet at the end of a meal.

▶ Cactus grows in the *desert.*
The Smiths served chocolate cake for *dessert.*

DeSERT (with the accent on the second syllable) can also be a verb, meaning "to leave alone," "to abandon."

▶ Will his wife *desert* him?

discover, invent To *discover* is to learn about something that already exists, but that people did not know about.
To *invent* is to create something new.

▶ Once humans *discovered* that round objects roll easily, they could then *invent* the wheel.

e.g., i.e.

E.g. is an abbreviation for the Latin words *exempli gratia,* meaning "as an example."
I.e. is an abbreviation for the Latin words *id est,* meaning "it is" or "that is."

▶ Southeast Asia has many fruits that are not common in the United States (*e.g.,* rambutans, durians, and loquats).
The person who first complained (*i.e.,* George Williamson) should be responsible for taking action.

emigrate, immigrate

Emigrate means "to leave one country to settle in another."
Immigrate means "to enter and settle in a country where you were not born."

▶ My parents *emigrated* from Poland and *immigrated* to the United States.

enthuse, be enthusiastic

Enthuse is not generally accepted; *be enthusiastic* should always be used instead.

▶ I am *enthusiastic* about the music of John Coltrane.

etc., and etc.

Etc. is an abbreviation for the Latin words *et cetera,* meaning "and others." Because *etc.* already includes *and,* do not put an additional *and* before it.
Etc. tends to be used too often simply to avoid thinking through the end of a list. Use *etc.* only when it has a clear and specific meaning.

▶ Gathered at the meeting were the college president, deans, teachers, students, *etc.*

everyone, every one

See *anyone, any one.*

farther, further

Farther usually refers to an additional physical distance, while *further* usually refers to additional nontangible amounts.

▶ The *farther* Caroline traveled away from her home, the *further* she felt on her own.

few, fewer, little, less

See *amount, number.*

former, latter

Former means "the first of two people or things."
Latter means "the second of two people or things."

▶ Barbara and Tina both passed; the *former* got an A and the *latter,* a C.

go and, go to, try and, try to, be sure and, be sure to

Go and, try and, and *be sure and* are all incorrect. Use *go to, try to,* and *be sure to.*

▶ Sam must *go to* pay his parking ticket.
You must *be sure to* turn out the lights when you leave.

good, well

Good is an adjective; it describes nouns only.
Well is usually an adverb and so describes verbs, but when it refers to health it can be an adjective and describe nouns.

▶ A *good* dinner warms my heart and fills my stomach.
Mr. Phibbs cooks *well.*
She was sick, but now she is *well.*

had ought, ought

Had ought is incorrect. Use only *ought.*

▶ I *ought* to be careful when I walk home late at night.

healthful, healthy

Healthful means "full of those things that make people healthy."
Healthy means "having good health."

▶ Despite Kean Hao's *healthful* diet, he did not look or feel *healthy.*

in, into

In means "entirely within a space."
Into implies entering the space.

▶ Six people were already *in* the small car when Bob, Jack, Jesse, and Mike tried to get *into* it, too.

infer, imply

Infer means "to conclude something from hints or evidence."
Imply means "to state something indirectly by giving hints."

▶ I *infer* from the report that Smith was doing a poor job.
The report *implies* that Smith was doing a poor job.

irregardless, regardless

Irregardless is wrong; use only *regardless,* which means "despite."

▶ The governor vowed to improve the schools *regardless* of the expense.

its, it's

Its is the ownership form of *it.*
It's is a short form of *it is.*

▶ The wolf circled around *its* victim.
This hat may be ugly, but *it's* the latest fashion.

lay, lie

Lay means "to place, put, or prepare."
Lie means "to stretch oneself out flat" or "to be located."
Check the list of irregular verbs on pages 79, 81–83 for past and perfect forms.

▶ Let me *lay* this package on the table.
Let me *lie* down and take a nap.
The town *lies* north of Boston.

learn, teach

Learn means "to gain knowledge."
Teach means "to give knowledge."

▶ Vera *learned* to count to ten, but then she forgot.
Will you *teach* me how to play chess?

leave, let

Leave means "to depart" or "to cause to remain."
Let means "to permit."

▶ The students wanted to *leave,* but the teacher wouldn't *let* them.
Grandpa made us *leave* our boots on the porch; he refused to *let* us track mud into the house.

loose, lose, loss

Loose is an adjective that means "not tight."
Lose is a verb that means "to misplace."
Loss is a noun that means "a thing no longer in one's possession."

▶ My watchband is *loose.*
I hope I don't *lose* the watch because it would be an expensive *loss.*

maybe, may be	*Maybe* (one word) means "perhaps." *May be* (two words) is a verb form.
	▶ *Maybe* the dogs will stop barking all night, but it *may be* that we will have to notify the police.
mine, mines	*Mines* is wrong; use only *mine* to mean "belonging to me."
	▶ The truth may be *mine,* but the power to decide is yours.
moral, morale	*Moral* means "ethical" or "a lesson at the end of a story." *Morale* means "the spirit or mood of a person or group of people."
	▶ The *moral* of this story is that one should always behave *morally.* Our team's *morale* was low after we lost the game.
much, many	See *amount, number.*
must have, must of	See *of, have.*
of, have	*Of* is often incorrectly used for *have* with verb forms such as *could, should, must, may,* and *ought.* Use *could have, should have, must have, may have,* and *ought to have* instead.
	▶ The store owner *should have* given you your money back.
passed, past	*Passed* is the past tense of the verb "to pass." *Past* is what happened before now.
	▶ In the *past,* I never could have *passed* a chocolate chip cookie without eating it.
prejudice, prejudiced	*Prejudice* is a noun that means "the holding of negative preconceived judgments about people." *Prejudiced* is an adjective that describes people or groups holding this attitude.
	▶ *Prejudice* will exist as long as some people remain *prejudiced.*

| principal, principle | *Principal* means "first" or "person with highest rank." |
| | *Principle* means "a basic truth or assumption." |

▶ The *principal* of the school spoke to Jason.
We must follow the *principle* that all men and women are born free.

quiet, quit, quite	*Quiet* is an adjective that means "without a sound."
	Quit is a verb that means "to stop doing something."
	Quite is an adverb that mean "very."

▶ *Quite* politely our neighbors asked us to be *quiet* and *quit* making noise.

| raise, rise | *Raise* means "to lift." |
| | *Rise* means "to go up." |

▶ Ms. Ramirez *raises* her eyebrows.
Ms. Ramirez' eyebrows *rise* when she is angry.

| respectfully, respectively | *Respectfully* means "with great respect." |
| | *Respectively* means "in the same order." |

▶ The private spoke to the general *respectfully.*
Paula, Diana, and David are twelve, seven, and five years old, *respectively.*

| set, sit | *Set* means "to put." |
| | *Sit* means "to be seated." |

▶ Have you *set* the clock ahead for daylight-saving time?
All the speakers will *sit* on the stage.

| should have, should've, should of | See *of, have.* |

| someone, some one | See *anyone, any one.* |

sometime, some time, sometimes	*Sometime* (one word) means "at an unspecified time."
	Some time (two words) is an amount of time.
	Sometimes means "now and then."

▶ The plumbers will finish the job *sometime,* but I don't know when.

Last summer I spent *some time* in Arkansas.
Sometimes James laughs so loudly the neighbors upstairs complain.

than, then

Than is used for comparisons.
Then is used to show the order of events in time.

▶ Oranges are sweeter *than* lemons.
First make your bed; *then* throw out the garbage.

their, there, they're

Their is the ownership form of *they*.
There means "not here."
They're is short for *they are*.

▶ They gave *their* promise that the work would be done.
Put the package down over *there*.
They're packing the suitcases right now.

threw, through

Threw is the past tense of the verb "to throw."
Through means "between" or "down the middle."

▶ Pacho *threw* the football *through* the open window.

to, too, two

To means "in the direction of."
Too means "also" and "excessively."
Two is a number.

▶ Take these letters *to* the post office.
There are *too* many cars on the highway.
The boy sold only *two* bottles of soda.

want, won't

Want is a verb that means "to desire."
Won't is short for "will not."

▶ I *won't* think about what you *want* until you consider the consequences of your actions.

were, we're, where

Were is a past tense form of the verb "to be."
We're is a contraction for "we are."
Where signifies a place.

▶ The pieces *were* all assembled.
We're going to solve this mystery.
We must know *where* you have been.

who, which, that   *Who, which,* and *that* are pronouns (see **8**)
used to combine sentences (see **6c**).
Who refers to people only.
Which and *that* refer to things and events, but
not to people.

▶ The children *who* visited the zoo brought back
balloons.
The balloons *that* [or *which*] they brought back
were soon broken.

who's, whose   *Who's* is short for "who is."
Whose is the ownership form of *who* and is
usually followed by a noun.

▶ *Who's* in charge here?
Whose bicycle is this?

would have,   See *of, have.*
would've would of

your, you're   *Your* means "belonging to you."
You're is short for "you are."

▶ *You're* certain that a balanced diet will improve
your health.

Mechanics

12

Punctuation

Marks of punctuation help make sentence meanings clearer.

12a STOPS AT THE END OF THE SENTENCE

12a(1) Exclamation Points

Use an exclamation point **!** to end an expression of strong feeling.

> Ah**!** I am in love**!** I am in love**!** I am in love**!**
> Don't you dare say that**!**
> I never want to see you again**!**

12a(2) Question Marks

Use a question mark **?** at the end of a direct question.

> When will I ever see you again**?**
> Why don't you leave me alone**?**
> Can this be love**?**

Do not use a question mark at the end of an indirect question.

> He asked if I was sick.

12a(3) Periods

Use a period **.** to end any sentence other than a direct question or an expression of strong feeling.

> I first saw her when she stepped onto the subway at Flatbush Avenue and Avenue K**.**

119

> She asked me how she could get to the Staten Island Ferry.
>
> I'll show you the way.
>
> Come with me.

Periods are also used to show words left out of quotations. Use three periods . . . to show words or sentences left out of the middle of a quotation. Use four periods . . . . to show words left out at the end of a quotation.

> We, the people of the United States, in order to form a more perfect Union . . . do ordain and establish this Constitution. . . .
>
> —Preamble to the Constitution

Periods are used after most abbreviations.

> Dr.   Jr.   B.A.   A.M.

12b   BREAKS IN THE MIDDLE OF THE SENTENCE

12b(1)   Commas

▶ Use a comma , to separate two sentences joined by *and, but, or, nor, for, so,* or *yet.* (See page 65.)

> I would have called, *but* I lost your phone number.

▶ Use a comma to separate items in a list.

> Myra packed her bags, said goodbye to her friends, bought an airplane ticket, and left for India.
>
> The tall, dark, handsome stranger wore boots, spurs, black pants, a black shirt, a red kerchief, and a black hat.

▶ Use a comma to set off long groups of words at the beginning of a sentence, particularly prepositional phrases (see page 97) and descriptive phrases (see page 70).

> Without money to buy a saddle, the stranger had to ride bareback.

▶ Use a comma to set off a dependent word group at the beginning (but not at the end) of a sentence. (See page 65.)

> *Because he wore tight boots,* the stranger had blisters.
>
> The stranger had blisters *because he wore tight boots.*

▶ Use commas to separate added-in words and phrases that are not part of the main idea of a sentence.

The stranger, *however,* used Band-Aids to lessen the pain.

▶ Use commas to separate out a descriptive dependent word group that is not needed to identify the person or thing described.

Sam Jones, *who knew the stranger from high school days,* opened the first drugstore west of the Mississippi. (You don't need the words *who knew the stranger . . .* to identify Sam Jones.)

Don't use a comma if the descriptive word group is needed to identify the person or thing.

The man *who knew the stranger from high school days* opened the first drugstore west of the Mississippi.

Here the words *who knew the stranger . . .* identify the man. (Which man? The man who knew the stranger from high school days.) Without those words, we don't know which man the writer is talking about. The phrase restricts the meaning of *man.*

▶ Use commas to set off the name of a person addressed.

Sam, is that you? I haven't seen you for years, *Sam.*

▶ Use a comma to separate phrases that might be confused.

Sam introduced the stranger to the saloonkeeper and the sheriff, and offered to give the stranger a room. (The comma clarifies that *and offered* goes with *introduced* rather than *saloonkeeper* and *sheriff.*)

▶ Use commas in titles, addresses, and dates.

Abdul Ali, M.D.
23 Walker Road, Toledo, OH
November 24, 1977

▶ Use commas with quotation marks. (See pages 127, 128.)

"Tell me what I should do," he said.
"Tell me," he said, "what I should do."

12b(2) Dashes

Use a dash — to interrupt a sentence dramatically and to put stress on words you've added. If you continue the main idea of the sentence after the interrupting phrase, use a second dash. A dash is longer than a hyphen; show it by typing two hypens next to each other: --.

> He fired the gun, and then—
>
> Afterward—*yes, he was a real criminal*—he didn't even bat an eyelash!

12b(3) Parentheses

Use parentheses ( ) to separate out material that breaks up the main idea of a sentence. Parentheses provide a stronger break than commas, but not as strong a break as dashes.

> John Smith (*also known as the Silver Straight-Arrow*) keeps watch over the city.

12b(4) Brackets

Use brackets [ ] to add your own words within a quotation.

> Ask not what your country can do for you; ask what you [*JFK was speaking to all Americans*] can do for your country.

12b(5) Colons

▶ The colon : means "as follows." Use a colon to introduce a long list.

> There are many comic book superheroes: *Superman, Batman, Wonder Woman, Green Arrow, Supergirl, Plastic Man, Captain Marvel, and others.*

Remember: the words before the colon should be a complete sentence. If the list completes the sentence, the colon is probably not needed.

WRONG	Two animal superheroes are: Mighty Mouse and Manfred the Wonder Dog.
RIGHT	Two animal superheroes are Mighty Mouse and Manfred the Wonder Dog.

RIGHT   There are two animal superheroes: Mighty Mouse
                         and Manfred the Wonder Dog.

▶ Use a colon to introduce a final word, phrase, or example that
  shows the meaning or result of the sentence.

Superheroes always manage to save themselves: *all superheroes are
immortal.*

▶ Use a colon in the greeting of a formal business letter and in
  separating hours, minutes, and seconds.

Dear Ms. Bulbenkian:
The time is exactly 7:36 A.M.

12b(6) Semicolons

▶ Use a semicolon ; to separate two sentences joined together
  without any linking words. (See page 64.)

Baseball used to be the national sport of the United States; football
has now replaced it.

▶ Use a semicolon to separate two sentences joined by the linking words *therefore, however, thus, moreover,* or the linking
  phrases *for example, in fact, in any case, on the other hand.*

I can afford the new car; *on the other hand,* I don't really need it.

▶ Use a semicolon instead of a comma to separate items in a list
  when there are commas within the items. The semicolon will
  make the separations clearer and prevent confusion.

We invited Harold, the butcher; Maxine, the dentist; Greg, the
teacher; Joe, the construction worker; Violet, the factory owner; and
Debbie, the landlord.

12c OTHER PUNCTUATION

12c(1) Apostrophes

▶ Use an apostrophe ' followed by an *s* to show ownership in
  words that do not end in *s* or *z*. It makes no difference whether
  the words are singular or plural.

Bill's house, Gloria's camera, the children's games, the man's car, the women's movement

▶ Use only the apostrophe when the word already ends in *s* or *z*.

Iris' temper, the ladies' magazine, the Joneses' house, Mrs. Ramirez' car

Do not use an apostrophe to make the plural of any word except for the special cases discussed below. *Spoon's* means "belonging to the spoon," not "more than one spoon."

Do not use apostrophes with pronouns that show ownership (see **8d**). *It's* means "it is," not "belonging to it." Use *its* to show ownership.

▶ Use an apostrophe to show missing letters in contractions.

don't (short for *do not*)
I'd (short for *I would* or *I had*)

▶ Use an apostrophe to make the plural of letters, numbers, abbreviations, and signs.

In advanced math there were two A's, eight B's, fifteen C's, six D's, and three F's.

12c(2) Hyphens

▶ Use a hyphen - to join some compound words together.

a three-month-old baby   a cross-reference

Check a dictionary to find which words should be written with hyphens.

▶ Use a hyphen to separate starting and ending numbers, dates, and scores.

pages 37-52   1974-1976   The Mets beat the Dodgers 4-3.

▶ Use a hyphen to break a long word at the end of a line. Be sure to break the word only between syllables. Check the dictionary to find the exact syllables of any word.

poly-   choles-
unsaturated   terol

PUNCTUATION REVIEW

. To end sentences and abbreviations:

Dr. Smith called.

? To end direct questions:

What time is it?

! To show surprise or strong emotion:

I don't believe it!

, To separate words, phrases, and sentences in a series:

apples, oranges, pineapples, and bananas

They ate, they drank, and they danced.

To set off opening phrases and dependent word groups:

While he was angry, he was difficult to talk to.

To separate out words and phrases not part of the main idea of the sentence:

Gene, *on the other hand,* got all the laughs.

To separate out phrases that do not restrict the meaning of nouns:

Fran, *the teacher's pet,* got all the answers right.

To set off the name of a person you are addressing:

Mary, how have you been?

To use in titles, dates, addresses:

Allen Schwartz, M.D.   June 30, 1945
Elk, California

— To interrupt a sentence and to emphasize added-in phrases:

Phil——*our last hope*——came to bat.

( ) To separate interrupting material:

Candy Jones (*of the prominent Jones family*) invited me to a party.

[ ] To add your own words in a quotation:

"Four score [*that means eighty*] and seven years ago. . . ."

: To introduce a long list:

There are five people here: *Joyce, Tom, Roz, Dom, and Joan.*

; To join two complete sentences together without using a connecting word:

Jack went to the theatre; Rachel went to the ball game.

' To show ownership:

Karen's shoes

To show contractions:

don't

- To join words together:

a six-year-old child

To break words into syllables at the end of a line:

ampli-
fication

___ To show that titles of long works, foreign words, emphasized words, and words discussed as words should be in italics (see Chapter 17):

Love Story (printed as *Love Story*)

" " To show exact quotations (see **13a**):

"Never," I said.

To show titles of short works (see **13d**):

"Sweet Little Sixteen"

13

Quotation Marks

13a DIRECT QUOTATIONS

Enclose the exact words of a speaker or writer within double quotation marks " ". If you use a phrase such as *he says* with a quotation, use the following models for punctuation:

> He said, "I cannot understand what you want of me."
>
> "I cannot understand," he said, "what you want of me."
>
> "I cannot understand what you want of me," he said.

Quotation marks always come in pairs; make sure every time you open a quotation with quotation marks, you close it with quotation marks at the end. If a direct quotation is more than a paragraph long, put quotation marks only at the beginning of each paragraph to remind the reader that the quotation is continuing. Do not use closing quotation marks until the end of the last paragraph of the quotation. If you are writing dialogue, you must start a new paragraph each time a different person speaks.

13b LONG DIRECT QUOTATIONS

In a research paper, do not use quotation marks for a quotation longer than fifty words. Instead, skip a line, indent each line of the quotation five typewriter spaces, or one-half inch, and single-space the quotation.

> Ernest Hemingway writes in a language that is very
>
> simple; yet, at the same time, it captures the reader's
>
> attention by always stating less than the writer really
>
> means. Here, from "On the Quai at Smyrna," is an

example of such understatement:

> The strange thing was, he said, how they screamed at midnight. I do not know why they screamed at that time. We were in the harbor and they were all on the pier and at midnight they started screaming. We used to turn the searchlight on them to quiet them. That always did the trick.

13c   QUOTATIONS WITHIN QUOTATIONS

Use single quotation marks ' ' to show a quotation within a quotation.

Jean said, "Eric said to me. 'You'd better not be late to class!' "

13d   TITLES OF SHORT WORKS

Use quotation marks for titles of short works, such as poems, short stories, songs, and television and radio programs.

"The Lady with a Lap Dog"   "St. Louis Blues"

(For titles of major works, see **17a**).

13e   QUOTATION MARKS WITH OTHER MARKS OF PUNCTUATION

Periods and commas go inside quotation marks.

Abner said, "Hello."

Question marks and exclamation points go inside the quotation marks if they are part of the quotation. If not, they are placed outside the quotation marks.

Sarah asked, "How are you, Abner?"

Abner answered. "I'm angry. Did Jay really say, 'Abner is a turkey'?"

Will Abner beat Jay up for saying "Abner is a turkey"?

Colons and semicolons go outside the quotation marks.

Sarah said, "I really don't know"; she knew better than to get involved in the fight between her two brothers.

14

Capitals

14a   SENTENCES AND QUOTATIONS

Use capitals

▶   for the first word in a sentence.

The child cried. **Her** mother kissed her.

▶   for the first spoken word in a quotation.

Leroy said, "**Let's** go."

14b   LETTERS

In a letter, capitalize

▶   the first letter of each word in the salutation.

Dear Sir:
Dear Ms. Stanley:

▶   the first letter of the first word (only) of the complimentary close.

Sincerely yours,
Yours truly,

14c   PROPER NAMES

Capitalize actual names of specific people, places, or things. More general words should not be capitalized, even when they identify individual people, places, or things.

129

14c(1)   Geographical Names

Pikes Peak	that mountain
Rhine River	a river in our state
Portland, Phoenix	our city
Lake Erie	a nearby lake

14c(2)   Streets, Buildings, Businesses, Organizations

Thomson Avenue, Lincoln Road	a wide avenue
East 96 Street, Linden Boulevard	a house on that street
Woolworth Building	that building
Marshall Field's Department Store	a large store
Ford Motor Company	a car company
First Baptist Church	the church

14c(3)   Schools, School Subjects, and Classes

Wichita State College	my college
Seaford High School	this high school
Chinese, English, Spanish	languages
Mathematics 11.1, History 18	mathematics, history
Brewster College Freshman Class	the freshman class

14c(4)   Seasons, Months, Days of the Week, Holidays

April, March, October	winter, spring, summer, fall
Tuesday, Saturday	today
the Fourth of July, Labor Day	my birthday

14c(5)   Directions and Special Regions

Southeast Asia	the northwest corner
She lives in the West.	Walk east on Main Street
I came from the South.	Drive south on the parkway.

14c(6)   Titles of Books, Newspapers, Magazines, Poems, Plays, Movies, TV Shows, Songs, Students' Compositions

Capitalize the first, last, and all other important words.

Independence Day	a frightening movie
"The X-Files"	my favorite TV show

"The Raven"   this poem
"An Embarrassment"   the short story

14c(7)   Historical Events

Revolutionary War   a long war
the Boxer Rebellion   a rebellion
the Boston Tea Party   a meeting
the Emancipation   a decree, a law
    Proclamation

14c(8)   Flowers, Trees, Animals, Games

Do not capitalize the names of flowers, trees, animals, or games.

carnation, maple, horse, soccer

14c(9)   Nationalities, Races, and Religions

Mexican, Chinese   a national holiday
Asian   black, white
Roman Catholic, Lutheran   a church member
Jewish, Protestant   an orthodox believer
God, the Bible   tribal gods, biblical
in His [God's] wisdom   a holy man

14c(10)   People's Names and Titles

Charles   the man
Anna Marino   the woman
President Gomez   the president of the college
Dr. Williams   my professor
President Roosevelt   president of the country
Representative Kono   the representative from Oregon

14c(11)   Relatives

Capitalize when the word of relation is used as a name.

Aunt Adele   my aunt
Uncle Hy   Dad's brother
I saw Dad.   I saw my dad.

15

Numbers

15a   FIGURES

In writing sentences that call for figures, spell out the figure if it takes two words or fewer; otherwise, use numerals.

eighty-five tons	687 tons
in *two thousand* years	in 350 years
twenty dollars	$22.15
one-eighth	52 $\frac{1}{8}$

15a(1)   Figures in Series

Be consistent if you need to write a series of figures. Use either words *or* numerals, not both together.

> *two* books, *four* pencils, *ten* crayons
> 218 lbs. of cement, 14 lbs. of nails, 116 bags of sand

15a(2)   Figures at the Beginning of the Sentence

Spell out any figure that starts a sentence.

> *Four thousand* cattle lay dead.

If you want to use numerals, rewrite the sentence so the figure does not come first.

> They killed 4,828 cattle.

15a(3)   Very Large Figures

Spell out large round numbers, unless you want to stress them—then use numerals.

eight billion dollars   OR $8 *billion*   OR $8,000,000,000
16.5 *million*   OR   16,500,000

15b   ADDRESSES

Use numerals in addresses.

1218 Remsen Avenue
Massapequa, NY 11758
Highway 101

If the name of a street is a number, you may spell out the number if it is below ten.

168 *Fifth* Avenue   OR   168 5th Avenue

But:

218 East 98 Street   OR   East 98th Street

15c   TIMES

Use numerals for telling time.

6 P.M., 4:30 A.M., 7:00 A.M.

Before the word *o'clock,* write out the figure.

ten o'clock in the morning

15d   PERCENTAGES

Use numerals to show percentages or decimal figures.

92%, a 2.7-mile drive, .37 of an inch

15e   DATES

Use numerals with dates.

1860–1865
June 28, 1973   (NOT June 28th, 1973)

But:

> the *fifth* of March, October *first*, the *twentieth* century, the *twenties*

15f FIGURES THAT SHOW ORDER

In general write out numbers that end in *th, nth, st, nd,* and *rd.*

their *thirtieth* anniversary   (NOT their 30th anniversary)

15g PARTS OF A BOOK

Use numerals to show parts of a book.

Part II, Chapter 4, page 27, question 5

16

Abbreviations

Usually, people avoid abbreviations in formal writing. Some abbreviations, however, are all right to use. Abbreviations usually need periods after them. The list here will help you decide when and how to abbreviate.

16a TITLES

Abbreviate titles that go before someone's full name. Don't abbreviate titles used without someone's name.

Dr. Rita Stark   I saw the *doctor.*
Mr. Jacob T. Wildwood   He wanted to be called *mister.*
Ms. Marion Arlin

Abbreviate titles or degrees used after someone's name. Don't abbreviate *professor, senator,* or *general* before last names alone.

Lionel Chase, *A.A., B.A.*   *General* Bradley
Blanche Jones, *Ph.D.*   *Professor* Hoban
Wilbur T. Washington, *Jr., M.D.*   *Senator* Ortiz

16b PARTS OF COMPANY NAMES

Abbreviate words and symbols used as parts of company names.

R & S Davis, *Inc.; P.* Bruce and Sons, *Ltd.*

16c PEOPLE'S NAMES

Do not abbreviate people's names.

> Thomas (NOT Thos.), Charles (NOT Chas.)

16d COMPANIES AND GOVERNMENT AGENCIES

Abbreviate the names of companies, government agencies, and other organizations that are well known.

> UNICEF, NATO, NBC, FBI

16e SCHOOL SUBJECTS

Do not abbreviate names of school subjects.

> economics (NOT econ.), mathematics (NOT math.), psychology (NOT psych.)

16f LATIN WORDS

Abbreviate certain Latin words used in writing.

> *i.e.* (that is); *e.g.* (for example); *viz.* (namely); *etc.* (and so forth); *re* (concerning)

16g SYMBOLS USED WITH WORDS

Some symbols are useful in tables or rough notes, but they should not be used with words in formal writing.

> and (NOT &); number (NOT #); without (NOT w/o)

16h ABBREVIATIONS OR SYMBOLS USED WITH NUMBERS

Use abbreviations or symbols for certain words when they appear with numbers.

> A.M. OR a.m. (5:22 A.M.); P.M. OR p.m. (8:00 p.m.)
> A.D., B.C. (A.D. 68; 2000 B.C.)
> No. OR no. (No. 15)
> \$, ¢ (\$15.27, 32¢)

16i MONTHS AND DAYS

Do not abbreviate the names of months and days.

> My birthday is in *April.*
> On *Tuesday* he arrived.
> *Friday, November 23*

17

Italics

Italics are slanted print. When using a typewriter or writing longhand, underline words that should be in italics.

17a TITLES OF MAJOR WORKS

Italicize (underline) titles of books, magazines, movies, plays, record albums, works of art, ships, and the like.

> *Moby Dick, Sports Illustrated, Star Wars, Hamlet, Tommy,* the *Mona Lisa,* the *Titanic*

(For titles of short works, see **13d.**)

17b FOREIGN WORDS

Italicize (underline) foreign words.

> In Spanish, *hasta la vista* means the same as *au revoir* in French: "until we see each other again."

Note: Many foreign words have become accepted as English words and do not need italics. For example,

> Eating too many blintzes, tacos, and pizzas will give you indigestion.

Check a dictionary to see whether a foreign word is now accepted as an English word.

17c   WORDS, LETTERS, AND NUMBERS USED AS SUCH

Italicize (underline) words, letters, or numbers when discussing them as words, letters, or numbers.

The word *grubby* originally came from the name for certain insect larvae, grubs.

17d   WORDS THAT NEED EMPHASIS

Italicize (underline) occasional words that need emphasis.

That is absolutely *disgusting.*

Remember: do not use italics for emphasis too often. Make sure you have a good reason when you do use them.

18

Spelling

18a SPELLING CORRECTLY

You are not alone if you find it difficult to spell correctly or if you often misspell words. Each person finds different words difficult to spell. The best way to improve your spelling is to notice which words *you* misspell. Keep a list of the correct spellings for those words and keep reviewing them. Some commonly misspelled words are presented in section **18b.**

Several other things may also help improve your spelling. Many misspellings occur through carelessness or typographical mistakes, so careful proofreading will help you catch errors before you turn in your written work (see **1d(2).** (Many writing programs for computers have tools built in to help you check your spelling, although the programs may not catch all errors.) Two or more English words that sound the same or nearly the same may have different spellings. Becoming aware of words that sound alike (homonyms) and words that sound almost alike (near homonyms) will also help your spelling (see **18c**). Some standard rules can also help you figure out how to spell certain words (see **18d** through **18h**). Finally, if you are unsure of the spelling of any word, you should always check a dictionary (see **18i**).

18b WORDS OFTEN MISSPELLED

The words in the following list are commonly misspelled by a number of people. Go over these words to make sure you know how to spell them. Study those you have difficulty with. The trouble spots are printed in darker type.

acc**omm**odate	dis**c**ipline	existence
analysis	dis**g**usted	forty
analy**z**e	emb**arrass**	fourth
benefited	envir**on**ment	g**u**arantee

license	play**wright**	signifi**cance**
lonely	pre**ce**de	simil**ar**
loo**se**	pre**ferr**ed	speak
lo**s**ing	privi**le**ge	spee**ch**
ne**cess**ary	profe**ssor**	stren**gth**
o**cc**asion	pursue	suc**cee**d
o**cc**u**rr**ed	recognize	vill**ain**
o**pp**ose	**rhyth**m	writing

18c   HOMONYMS AND NEAR HOMONYMS

In order to spell correctly, you need to recognize words that sound alike but that are spelled differently and have different meanings. Section **11g** on words commonly confused contains a number of homonyms and near homonyms. The following list contains other homonyms and near homonyms that may cause spelling difficulties. If you are unsure of the meaning of any of the words listed below, check the dictionary.

accept, except	loose, lose
adapt, adopt	passed, past
advice, advise	personal, personnel
affect, effect	presence, presents
altar, alter	principal, principle
brake, break	raise, raze
buy, by	stationary, stationery
capital, capitol	than, then
cite, sight, site	their, there, they're
conscience, conscious	to, too, two
complement, compliment	weather, whether
formally, formerly	whose, who's
its, it's	your, you're
lead, led	

18d   THE *IE* RULE

▶   The letter *i* usually comes before *e*:

chief, pierce, field

▶   After the letter *c,* the *e* usually comes first:

ceiling, perceive, receive

▶   If the sound of the two letters is ā (to rhyme with *say*), we usually write *ei*:

neighbor, sleigh, weigh, eight, vein

▶ Exceptions (memorize them!):

either, height, neither, seize, their, weird

18e FINAL *E*

Words that end in *e* sometimes change when a suffix (an ending) is added.

▶ If the suffix begins with a vowel, drop the *e* at the end of the word and add the suffix.

come + ing = coming
excite + able = excitable

▶ Keep the *e* at the end of the word if the suffix starts with a consonant.

hope + less = hopeless
advertise + ment = advertisement

▶ Exceptions:

notice + able = noticeable
courage + ous = courageous
argue + ment = argument
dye + ing = dyeing
true + ly = truly
judge + ment = judgment

18f DOUBLED LETTERS

When a word changes its form (from *run* to *running,* for example), its last letter is sometimes doubled.

▶ If the word is one syllable long, if it ends in a consonant, and if one vowel comes before the consonant, double the last letter before adding the ending.

run + ing = running
plan + ed = planned

▶ If the word ends in two consonants, or if there are two vowels before the final consonant, do not double the last letter before adding the ending.

grasp + ing = grasping
lead + ing = leading

▶ In two-syllable words, double the last letter if

1. it is a consonant.
2. only one vowel comes before the consonant.
3. you accent the last syllable when you say the word.

For example:

prefer (pronounced *preFER*) + ed = preferred

But:

retail (pronounced *REtail*) + ing = retailing (two vowels, no accent)

18g   FINAL *Y*

Words that end in *y* sometimes change when a suffix is added.

▶ If the letter before the final *y* is a consonant, change the *y* to *i*.

try + es = tries
reply + ed = replied

▶ If the letter before the final *y* is a vowel, do not change *y*.

stay + ed = stayed

▶ If the ending you add begins with *i*, do not change the *y*.

reply + ing = replying

18h   PLURALS

Plurals are formed in many ways.

18h(1)   Regular Plurals

▶ Add *s* to most words.

book, books; dollar, dollars; table, tables

▶ Add *es* to words ending in *ch, sh, ss, x, z.*

bench, benches; wish, wishes; dress, dresses; box, boxes

▶ If a word ends in *y* and a consonant comes before the *y*, change *y* to *i* and add *es*.

fly, flies; country, countries

▶ If a word ends in *y* and a vowel comes before the *y*, add *s*. Don't change anything.

day, days; turkey, turkeys

▶ If a word ends in *o* and the *o* comes after a vowel, most of the time you add an *s*.

radio, radios; duo, duos

▶ If a word ends in *o* and the *o* comes after a consonant, add *es*.

potato, potatoes; tomato, tomatoes

Exceptions:

soprano, sopranos; piano, pianos; auto, autos

▶ Some words ending in *f* or *fe* change *f* to *v* before adding *s* or *es*.

elf, elves; knife, knives; half, halves; wife, wives

▶ Some words ending in *f* or *fe* keep the *f* in the plural form.

belief, beliefs

18h(2)   Words with Special Changes

Many words form plurals by changing their spelling completely.

tooth, teeth; goose, geese
man, men; woman, women
child, children; ox, oxen
mouse, mice

The dictionary will tell you which spelling to choose for the plural form.

18h(3)   Words That Don't Change

Some words are the same whether singular or plural:

sheep   deer   series

Some words are always plural:

> people   cattle   rice

18h(4)   Words with Special Endings

Some words—especially words that come from foreign languages—form plurals in unusual ways.

> curriculum, curricula; medium, media; criterion, criteria
> crisis, crises; analysis, analyses
> alumna, alumnae

18h(5)   Combined Words

Words made by putting together two or more words form plurals by adding *s* to the base word.

> mother-in-law, mothers-in-law
> editor-in-chief, editors-in-chief

18h(6)   Letters, Numbers, and Abbreviations

Use an apostrophe and *s* (**'s**) to show the plural of a letter, number, or abbreviation.

> There are two *c*'s and two *m*'s in *accommodate*.
> Don't use *etc.*'s in your writing.
> All the 3's were mistyped as 8.
> P.O.W.'s

18i   USING A DICTIONARY FOR SPELLING AND MEANING

A dictionary contains a great deal of information about words—from their correct pronunciation to their history—as you can see in the labeled sample from the *American Heritage Dictionary* on page 147. Most dictionaries provide an introduction that explains the material covered inside. People use dictionaries most often to check the spellings and meanings of words.

18i(1) Checking Spelling

In each dictionary entry the main word is spelled in large dark type, and other forms of the word are spelled in smaller dark type. Listed on the sample page after the main entry *salesman*, for example, are the forms *salesmanship* and *saleswoman*. For the word *sake* (second entry), a second or alternate spelling is given, *saki*. So once you have found the word entry, you have the spelling for the word and any alternate forms.

The problem is finding the entry for a word you don't know how to spell. Words in a dictionary are arranged in alphabetical order. If you know the first few letters of the word you are looking for, you should have no problem finding it. If you are not sure of the first few letters, try the spelling you think most likely. If you still can't locate it, try all other letter combinations that might sound like your word. For example, if you did not know how to spell the word *crime*, you might have to check out all these possible spellings before you came to the right one: cryme, kryme, khryme, chryme, krime, creim, crime.

Also notice where dots mark the syllable breaks in the entry words. For example, the word *salamander* is broken into *sal•a•man•der*. Knowing these syllable breaks is important if you need to break a long word at the end of a line. Break words only at the ends of syllables, as discussed in **12c(2)**.

18i(2) Checking Word Meanings

Dictionary entries give the most important or most frequent meaning of a word first, with other meanings following in order of decreasing use. Meanings are also grouped according to the way the word is used grammatically. For example, the word *sail* has more than one meaning as both a noun and a verb. The most important meaning for the noun is the piece of cloth used to catch the wind on a boat. The most important meaning for the verb is to move on water, using a sail.

Sometimes the dictionary will give a synonym (abbreviated *Syn.*)— that is, a word that has the same meaning as the entry word. You can find many more synonyms in a thesaurus or dictionary of synonyms. However, be careful when you replace a word with its synonym in your writing, because the two words may have slightly different shades of meaning (see **11e**). If a synonym has the wrong shade of meaning, it will not fit your sentence.

Guide words

Main entries

Pronunciation

Part of speech

Special forms and spellings

Meaning

History of the word

Pronunciation key

safeguard / salient   620

assuring unmolested passage, as through enemy lines.
safe•guard (săf'gärd') *n.* A precautionary measure or device. —*v.* To insure the safety of; protect.
safe•keep•ing (săf'kē'pĭng) *n.* Protection; care.
safe•ty (săf'tē) *n., pl.* **-ties. 1.** Freedom from danger or injury. **2.** Any of various protective devices. **3.** *Football.* **a.** A play in which the offensive team downs the ball behind its own goal line. **b.** A defensive back closest to his own goal line.
safety match. A match that can be lighted only by being struck against a chemically prepared friction surface.
safety pin. A pin in the form of a clasp, having a sheath to cover and hold the point.
saf•fron (săf'rən) *n.* **1.** The dried orange-yellow stigmas of a kind of crocus, used to color and flavor food and as a dye. **2.** Orange-yellow. [< Ar *za'farān.*] —**saf'fron** *adj.*
sag (săg) *v.* **sagged, sagging. 1.** To sink or bend downward, as from pressure or slackness. **2.** To droop. [Perh < Scand.] —**sag** *n.*
sa•ga (sä'gə) *n.* **1.** An Icelandic prose narrative of the 12th and 13th centuries. **2.** A long heroic narrative. [ON, a story, legend.]
sa•ga•cious (sə-gā'shəs) *adj.* Shrewd and wise. [< L *sagāx.*] —**sa•gac'i•ty** (-găs'ə-tē) *n.*
sage¹ (sāj) *n.* A venerable wise man. —*adj.* **sager, sagest.** Judicious; wise. [< L *sapere,* to be sensible, be wise.] —**sage'ly** *adv.*
sage² (sāj) *n.* **1.** An aromatic plant with grayish-green leaves used as seasoning. **2.** Sagebrush. [< L *salvia,* "the healing plant."]
sage•brush (sāj'brŭsh') *n.* An aromatic shrub of arid regions of W North America.
sag•it•tal (săj'ə-təl) *adj.* **1.** Of or like an arrow or arrowhead. **2.** Relating to the suture uniting the two parietal bones of the skull. [< L *sagitta,* arrow.] —**sag'it•tal•ly** *adv.*
Sag•it•ta•ri•us (săj'ə-târ'ē-əs) *n.* **1.** A constellation in the S Hemisphere. **2.** The 9th sign of the zodiac. [< L *sagittārius,* an archer, Sagittarius.]
sa•go (sā'gō) *n.* A powdery starch obtained from the trunks of an Asian palm. [Malay *sagu.*]
sa•gua•ro (sə-gwär'ō, sə-wär'ō) *n., pl.* **-ros.** Also **sa•hua•ro** (sə-wär'ō). A very large branching cactus of SW North America. [Mex Span.]
Sa•har•a (sə-hár'ə, -hǎ'rə). A desert of N Africa.
sa•hib (sä'ĭb) *n.* A title of respect for Europeans in colonial India, equivalent to *master* or *sir.* [Hindi *sāhib,* master, lord.]
said (sĕd) *p.t. & p.p.* of **say.** —*adj.* Aforementioned.
Sai•gon (sī-gŏn'). The capital of South Vietnam. Pop. 1,400,000.
sail (sāl) *n.* **1.** A length of shaped fabric that catches the wind and propels or aids in maneuvering a vessel. **2.** A sailing ship. **3.** A trip in a sailing craft. **4.** Something resembling a sail. —*v.* **1.** To move across the surface of water by means of a sail. **2.** To travel by water

in a vessel. **3.** To start out on a voyage. **4.** To operate a sailing craft; navigate or manage (a vessel). **5.** To glide through the air; soar. [< OE *segl* < Gmc **seglam.*]
sail•boat (sāl'bōt') *n.* A small boat propelled by a sail or sails.
sail•fish (sāl'fĭsh') *n.* A large marine fish with a large dorsal fin and a spearlike projection from the upper jaw.
sail•or (sā'lər) *n.* **1.** One who serves in a navy or earns his living working on a ship. **2.** A straw hat with a flat top and brim.
saint (sānt) *n.* **1.** *Theol.* **a.** A person officially entitled to public veneration for extreme holiness. **b.** A human soul inhabiting heaven. **2.** A very holy or unselfish person. [< L *sanctus,* sacred.] —**saint'dom** *n.* —**saint'hood'** *n.*
saint•ly (sānt'lē) *adj.* **-lier, -liest.** Of or befitting a saint. —**saint'li•ness** *n.*
Saint-Saëns (săn-sänś'), **Camille.** 1835–1921. French composer.
saith (sĕth, sā'əth). *Archaic.* 3rd person sing. present indicative of **say.**
sake¹ (sāk) *n.* **1.** Purpose; motive: *for the sake of argument.* **2.** Advantage, benefit, or welfare. [< OE *sacu,* lawsuit. See **sāg-.**]
sa•ke² (sä'kē) *n.* Also **sa•ki.** A Japanese liquor made from fermented rice.
sa•laam (sə-läm') *n.* An Oriental obeisance performed by bowing low while placing the right palm on the forehead. [Ar *salām,* "peace."] —**sa•laam'** *v.*
sa•la•cious (sə-lā'shəs) *adj.* Lewd; bawdy. [< L *salāx,* fond of leaping, lustful.] —**sa•la'cious•ly** *adv.* —**sa•la'cious•ness, sa•lac'i•ty** (sə-lăs'ə-tē) *n.*
sal•ad (săl'əd) *n.* A dish usually consisting of raw green vegetables tossed with a dressing. [< VL **salāre,* to salt.]
sal•a•man•der (săl'ə-măn'dər) *n.* **1.** A small, lizardlike amphibian. **2.** A portable stove used to heat or dry buildings under construction. [< Gk *salamandra.*]
sa•la•mi (sə-lä'mē) *n.* A highly spiced and salted sausage. [< It *salame,* "salted pork."]
sal•a•ried (săl'ə-rēd) *adj.* Earning or yielding a regular salary.
sal•a•ry (săl'ə-rē, săl'rē) *n., pl.* **-ries.** A fixed compensation for services, paid on a regular basis. [< L *salārium,* orig "money given to Roman soldiers to buy salt."]
sale (sāl) *n.* **1.** The exchange of property or ownership for money. **2.** Demand; ready market. **3.** Availability for purchase: *on sale.* **4.** An auction. **5.** A special disposal of goods at lowered prices. [< OE *sala* < ON.] —**sal'a•ble, sale'a•ble** *adj.*
Sa•lem (sā'ləm). The capital of Oregon. Pop. 68,000.
sales•man (sālz'mən) *n.* A man employed to sell merchandise, insurance, etc. —**sales'man•ship'** *n.* —**sales'wom'an** *fem.n.*
sal•i•cyl•ic acid (săl'ə-sĭl'ĭk). A white crystalline acid, $C_7H_6O_3$, used in making aspirin. [< L *salix,* willow.]
sa•li•ent (sā'lē-ənt) *adj.* **1.** Projecting or jutting beyond a line. **2.** Striking; conspicuous. [< L *salīre,* to leap, jump.] —**sa'li•ence, sa'li•en•cy** *n.*

Index